DELHI, AGRA & RAJASTHAN

BY

MELISSA SHALES

Produced by
Thomas Cook Publishing

Written by Melissa Shales
Updated by Andrew Forbes/CPA Media
Original photography by Douglas Corrance
Updated photography by David Henley/CPA Media

Original design by Laburnum Technologies Pvt Ltd

Editing and page layout by Cambridge Publishing Management Lt●
Unit 2, Burr Elm Court, Caldecote CB3 7NU
Series Editor: Penny Isaac

Published by Thomas Cook Publishing
A division of Thomas Cook Tour Operations Limited
PO Box 227, The Thomas Cook Business Park,
Units 15–16, Coningsby Road,
Peterborough PE3 8SB, United Kingdom
E-mail: books@thomascook.com
www.thomascookpublishing.com
Tel: +44 (0)1733 416477

ISBN: 1-841574-81-3

Text © 2005 Thomas Cook Publishing
Maps © 2005 Thomas Cook Publishing
First edition © 2002 Thomas Cook Publishing
Second edition © 2005 Thomas Cook Publishing

Head of Thomas Cook Publishing: Chris Young
Project Editor: Linda Bass
Project Administrator: Michelle Warrington
DTP: Steven Collins

Printed and bound in Spain by: Grafo Industrias Gráficas, Basauri

Cover design by: Liz Lyons Design, Oxford.
Front cover credits: Left © Mark Sykes/Alamy; centre © Beren Patterson/Alamy; right © Indiapicture/Alamy.
Back cover credits: Left © TIM GRAHAM/Alamy; right © Thomas Cook Tour Operations Ltd.

C o n t e n t s

KEY TO MAPS
∿ City walks/fortifications
★ Start of walk/tour
▬ Railway station
i Tourist information
✈ Airport
▲ 1722m Mountain

Introduction

India has the ageing elegance of an ancient civilisation; she also has the raw and abrasive energy of a newly independent power. Heart-stopping beauty and spiritual fervour cloak abject poverty; physical squalor can hide the souls of saints. She will inflame and overpower the senses, bombarding them with sights, sounds and smells to feast upon, and also sicken. She is confusing and frustrating, inspiring and uplifting. You will return home enriched and bemused and, whether you loved or loathed the country, you will never be quite the same again.

Nothing here is ever what it seems. The tattiest building can hide inner walls inlaid with precious stones. The man in the cotton pyjama suit may be a clerk or a milkman or a cabinet minister. People weave pure silk, but prefer nylon as it is cheaper; Hinduism accepts making honest money as a sacred duty, but successful men freely give up all worldly goods and become wandering *sadhus*.

Delhi, capital of India, Agra, home of the Taj Mahal and Jaipur, capital of Rajasthan, together make up the **Golden Triangle** as three of India's most visited and fascinating cities. This book also includes all of Rajasthan, a corner of India as big as many European countries.

Until they joined India in 1949, there were 23 independent Rajput kingdoms, with a rich tradition of history, art, and architecture in great palace cities such as Udaipur, Jodhpur, and Jaisalmer. Rajasthan is also an area of great beauty, from the jungle-clad hills and lakes of the south, to the deserts of the north-west, where camels are as precious as life. Above all, the people, with their vibrant skirts, saris and turbans, heavy silver, and twirling moustaches, make the area unforgettable. A holiday here will never be totally comfortable, but it will be one of the greatest experiences of your life.

THOMAS COOK'S Delhi, Agra and Rajasthan

By 1870 Thomas Cook was selling steamer tickets to India (£50 First Class; journey time – 30 days). In 1873, teetotal Thomas Cook himself visited India during a world tour, spent an evening with the Temperance Society of the Agra garrison, and promised to send them a library of books to help with the boredom (lest they should succumb to drink). By 1880, the company was setting up guided tours across India – and tours for Indian residents to other areas of the world. The first ran over Easter, 1881. By 1887, they were advertising a wide range of itineraries including stops in Delhi, Agra, Jaipur and Ajmer. By 1891, the company had set up its first banking services in India, and by 1892 was publishing pamphlets with practical information and details of the major sights.

Spectacular camel parade during the Jaisalmer Desert Festival

Land and people

The area covered by this book falls mainly within the western half of the vast undulating plains of north India, at 200m to 400m above sea level. Delhi, a Union Territory, covering 1,483sq km, and Agra, the largest city in the massive state of Uttar Pradesh, lie within the outer limits of the Ganges basin, along its tributary, the Yamuna. Rajasthan (formerly Rajputana) covers 342,239sq km, and divides into two very different landscapes. The southeastern hills are lush, well-watered, and fertile, with heavy monsoons from July to September. The central Aravalli Hills (maximum height 670m) mark the edge of the Ganges watershed. Beyond them, the land is increasingly flat and arid, eventually melting into the burning sands of the great Thar Desert, with temperatures reaching a summer maximum of 50°C.

In many villages, the traditional system of watering the land is still used whereby yoked oxen draw water from deep wells

GREENING THE DESERT

The Indira Gandhi Nahar (canal) begins in the Punjab, at the Harrika Barrage at the confluence of the Sutlej and Beas rivers. On completion in 2005, it comprised a main 701-km long canal and nearly 9,500km of branches and minor tributaries. It supplies Himalayan water for drinking and industry, and irrigates an area of more than 187 million hectares. It has already halted the relentless expansion of the desert. Droughts and floods are being brought under control, and with the planting of new crops, Rajasthan's scrubby sands are slowly being transformed into a lush, green paradise. The resulting agriculture has more than paid for the project. The authorities have even designated an area as a Desert National Park, to preserve a slice of desert ecology for the future (see p142).

Population

India has the second largest population in the world, currently estimated at over one billion, of whom 70 per cent still live in rural areas. About 85 per cent are Hindu, and 11 per cent Muslim. There are also around 23 million Christians, 19 million Sikhs, 7 million Buddhists, 4 million Jains and a small number of Parsees (Zoroastrians, centred around Mumbai) and animist/pagan tribal groups. Delhi, with a population nearing 14 million, is India's third largest city. Around 2.8 million people live in Agra.

Rajasthan, with about 57 million people, is one of the poorer states in India, with 17 per cent of the population belonging to Scheduled Castes or untouchables, and 12 per cent classified as tribal or ethnic minorities. Most prominent among these are the Meenas and Bheels; smaller groups include nomads. The state still has one of the world's highest birth rates.

The average annual income is two-thirds that of India as a whole, although the literacy rate is now about 60 per cent.

Growth and economy

Delhi is a world-class capital, rapidly expanding in terms of physical and financial growth. Agra is a centre for heavy and light industry. Rajasthan has a relatively small industrial base. Most workers here still huddle in tiny craft workshops, producing fine carpets, jewellery and fabrics. Mining for marble, quartz and silver, as well as semi-precious stones, such as jasper and cornelian, has long been a prime source of its income. Village subsistence agriculture is being joined by an expansion of cash crops, such as pulses, sugar cane, cotton, and millet, thanks to irrigation schemes like the Indira Gandhi Canal. One of the biggest industries of all in the state is tourism.

The stark gravel plains of the Thar desert are interspersed with sandy dunes

History

8500 BC–3500 BC	Evidence of agricultural activity and settlement in the Indus Valley.
2500–1500 BC	The Harappa culture – encompassing the sites of Mohenjo Daro and Harappa – grows out of the earlier Indus Valley cultures. City dwellers, traders and builders are part of the first significant civilisation on the subcontinent.
1500–1000 BC	The first Aryans arrive from the Middle East, bringing with them the chariot, the Vedic religion (the precursor of Hinduism) and the caste system.
1000–500 BC	The Aryans move into the Ganges-Yamuna plains to establish small kingdoms. Buddhism is founded by Prince Siddhartha Gautam (the Buddha, c.563–483 BC), and Jainism by Mahavira (Vardhamana Jnatputra, c.540–468 BC), both in north India.
321–185 BC	The Maurya Dynasty is founded by Chandragupta. His grandson, Ashoka (c.268–231 BC), conquers almost the entire subcontinent to become India's first emperor. Repelled by the horrors of war, he embraces Buddhism, and spreads the message of non-violence through stone-inscribed edicts. Empire fragments on his death.
AD 320–535	Founding of the Gupta Empire in north India. It is a golden age of both arts and sciences, brought to an end by invading Huns. The area again dissolves into tiny kingdoms.
AD 606–647	Harshvardhan rules for 41 years over north India, including Nepal.
8th–11th centuries	In 711, the first Arab invasions bring Islam to north India. From about 750 onwards Hindu Rajput clans emerge from the west, and begin to build up real power across northwest India, although they remain fragmented into numerous small kingdoms who spend much of their time fighting each other (*see pp96–7*).
11th–12th centuries	Increasingly frequent Islamic incursions begun

by Mahmud of Ghazni culminate in a fierce campaign by the Turkish Sultan, Mohammed Ghori. In 1192 he defeats a group of Rajputs led by Prithviraj Chauhan and claims their territory, leaving a trusted slave, Qutbuddin Aibak, now ranked as a general, in Delhi as his governor.

1206–1526 In 1206 Ghori is killed, and Qutbuddin sets himself up as Sultan of Delhi, founding the Delhi Sultanate or 'Slave Dynasty'. A succession of dynasties follows, with Delhi a centre of prosperity and power for the first 150 years. Muslim rulers and the Hindu Rajputs battle it out for 320 years.

1398–9 The first Mongol invasion, led by Timur (Tamburlaine), heir of Genghis Khan, reduces the Delhi Sultans to control of only a tiny area around the city.

1469 Guru Nanak, founder of Sikhism, is born in the Punjab, north India.

1498 Vasco da Gama discovers the sea route to the East, landing on India's southwestern shores, and Europe begins to take an interest in India.

1526 Second Mongol invasion. Babur (ruler of a small kingdom in central Asia and a descendant of Genghis Khan) defeats the Sultan of Delhi, Ibrahim Lodi, to found the Mughal Dynasty (*see pp54–5*).

Muslim invaders are depicted in this 11th-century miniature

Emperor Jahangir holds a portrait of Akbar

In all, there were 17 Mughal emperors, of whom the first six were the greatest. Warriors, builders, garden lovers and patrons of the arts, they created a golden age of Indian culture, leaving north India its most enduring legacies – exquisite arts and crafts, the great forts of Delhi, Agra and Rajasthan and that most beautiful of buildings, the Taj Mahal (*see p60*). The dynasty survived until 1857 when the last Mughal emperor, Bahadur Shah II, was exiled by the British for his part in the Indian Mutiny.

Late 16th century	Emperor Akbar is crowned at the age of 13 in 1556. He astutely forms marriage and military alliances with some Rajput princes, subjects others to ferocious and prolonged warfare, and brings Rajputana into the Mughal Empire as a series of subject states. Only the Maharana of Udaipur holds out, in spite of the loss of his great fort of Chittorgarh, and flees to Udaipur which becomes his new capital (*see p128*).
1618	The British East India Company receives trading privileges from the Mughals in exchange for protecting their trade routes from the Portuguese. Over the next 50 years British influence gradually fans out across India.
18th century	The Mughal Empire begins to crumble following the death of Bahadur Shah in 1712. The Maratha Empire stretches north and east from the Deccan. The Mughals enlist their help against Afghan invaders who finally overpower them in 1761. Mughal power centres break up. By the end of the century, the subject Rajputs turn to Britain for help in getting rid of the Marathas. The ensuing treaties theoretically

restore Rajput independence, but in practice the principalities become British protectorates.

1773–74 The Regulating Act turns the East India Company into a British administrative agency. Warren Hastings is appointed the first Governor-General of British India. He offers several Indian princes military protection in exchange for various concessions – effectively setting up puppet states.

1799 Lord Wellesley (later to become the Duke of Wellington) leads a huge military campaign, conquering a great deal more of southern India.

1815–18 The final British conquest of the Marathas. Almost the entire subcontinent is now under the direct rule or 'influence' of the British Raj.

1857–58 The Indian Mutiny is sparked off in Meerut by a false rumour that bullets are stored in cow and pig fat, offending both Hindu and Muslim soldiers. The Rajputs ally themselves with the British. Intense fighting, atrocities, and sieges occur on both sides before the British finally gain control. The last Mughal, Bahadur Shah II, sides with the Mutineers. He is captured in the grounds of Humayun's tomb, tried for treason in the Red Fort, Delhi, and exiled to Burma. The British government buys out the East India Company, declaring India to be part of the British Empire, governed by a viceroy and an Indian Council.

1877 Queen Victoria is proclaimed Empress of India.

1885 The first nationalist stirrings. The Indian National Congress holds its first meeting in December.

1906 Foundation of the All-India Muslim League.

1911 The Great Durbar is held in Delhi in honour of King George V. Capital of British India transferred from Calcutta to Delhi.

Representatives of the East India Company

1914–18 Indian troops play an important role in World War I. All internal political disagreements are put on hold during this time. In 1915 the political activist Mohandas Karamchand Gandhi returns from South Africa to take part in the struggle for independence. The end of the war sees a new stirring of nationalist fervour.

1919 General Dyer fires on a nationalist protest in Amritsar, killing and injuring over 1,500 men, women, and children.

1920s National movement gathers strength; Gandhi propounds the theory of *swaraj* (self rule) and *satyagraha* (non-violent non-cooperation); all nationalist leaders spend time in prison. In 1927 Congress demands full independence.

February 1931 Sir Edwin Lutyens' planned city of New Delhi is officially inaugurated.

1932 Congress splits after Gandhi demands full political rights for the Harijans (untouchables).

1935–39 The Government of India Act aims to set up a federation of autonomous states with Dominion status. The first state elections in 1937 lead to a huge Congress majority.

1939–47 India is involved in World War II and Dominion status is put on hold. Militant leader Subhas Chandra Bose sets up a parallel Indian National Army. In 1940, the Muslim League demands a separate Muslim state. In 1942, Gandhi and Jawaharlal Nehru lead a

'Quit India' campaign, during which 1,000 people are killed and 60,000 arrested. Lord Mountbatten is appointed Viceroy in 1947 to oversee the transfer of power.

1947 On 15 August, India gains independence, with Nehru as first prime minister of India. Violent communal riots follow the migration of 13 million people across the new border of Pakistan and India. Up to one million people die.

January 1948 Gandhi is killed by a Hindu extremist.

1949–56 In exchange for retaining titles and the privy purse, the maharajas give up their power and lands and join the Indian Union.

1964–65 Jawaharlal Nehru dies in 1964. First Indian war with Pakistan over land disputes in 1965.

1971 Prime Minister Indira Gandhi abolishes the privy purses and royal titles, though many former rulers are still socially referred to as 'maharaja' and 'maharani'. Second Indo-Pakistan war. Pakistan is split; Bangladesh created.

1984 Indira Gandhi (prime minister 1966–77 and 1980–84) is assassinated by Sikh members of her bodyguard.

1991 Rajiv Gandhi, son of Indira, is killed by Tamil extremists near Chennai.

1995 Pakistan-backed militancy in Kashmir gathers momentum.

1998 The right-wing Bharatiya Janata Party (BJP) is elected to lead the new coalition government. In May, India tests nuclear bombs.

2004 In a surprise result, the Indian National Congress Party led by Sonia Gandhi wins the national elections. Manmohan Singh becomes India's new prime minister.

Gandhi – pictured here outside 10 Downing St – maintained good relations with the British

Governance

Land of diverse religions and regional groups, and a great disparity between the rich and poor, India has nevertheless sustained a democratic system since Independence that has survived violent protests, riots, internal terrorism and assassinations. There have been 13 general elections fought between an increasing number of political parties amidst reports of corruption and electoral rigging. Nevertheless, the Indian electorate remains firmly committed to governance by people's representation, and there has never been any suggestion of a military coup. There is freedom of press and speech, and the judiciary is independent and often outspoken. The Constitution is, on paper at least, one of the most liberal and idealistic in the world, although many aspects are widely ignored in favour of traditional custom or expediency.

Indira Gandhi, first female prime minister of India

The Constitution

India is a federal republic within the Commonwealth, with a written constitution that enshrines several high ideals, including universal suffrage, a ban on untouchability, equal rights for women and a declaration of human rights. There are two houses of parliament. The Lok Sabha (House of the People) has 545 members and represents the people as a whole, with 120 seats reserved for the Scheduled Castes and two nominated representatives of the Anglo-Indian population. The Rajya Sabha (Council of State) has 245 members, representing the Federal States. Each state then has its own Legislative Assembly or Vidhan Sabha. Central government controls defence, foreign affairs, currency, railways, post and ports. The states are responsible for education, agriculture, industry and the police. The prime minister, leader of the majority party, governs with the aid of a cabinet. The figurehead president has the right to intervene only if central or state government has collapsed.

Congress and the Nehru Dynasty

Since it was founded back in 1885, the Congress Party has been the over-whelmingly dominant force in the country's politics, remaining in power for over 45 years since 1947. For most of that time it has been led by a member of the Nehru family. In the 1920s, Motilal Nehru was co-author of a first draft constitution. In 1947, his son, Jawaharlal, became the country's first prime minister, ruling until his death in 1964. In 1966, his daughter, Indira

Gandhi, took over, remaining in power for all but three years, until she was assassinated in 1984. Within hours, her son, Rajiv, had been sworn in, remaining in office until 1989. In 1991, he was killed by Tamil separatists. Congress remained in power for several more years under PV Narasimha Rao, although its popularity waned. In 1998, following electoral losses, Rajiv Gandhi's wife, Sonia Gandhi, agreed to become Congress Party president in a bid to boost its flagging popularity.

The Bharatiya Janata Party (BJP)

Meanwhile, the right-wing Hindu nationalist party, the Bharatiya Janata Party (BJP) narrowly won the 1998 elections and formed a national coalition government. Pre-election promises included a commitment to Hindu fundamentalism, while early efforts at whipping up grassroots support involved numerous blatant displays of communalism, including destruction of a historic mosque at Ayodhya. One of the BJP's first major acts on gaining power was to run nuclear tests within a few miles of the Pakistani border. The Pakistanis ran their own test shortly afterwards, and the subcontinental arms race escalated.

By 2004 BJP popularity was in serious decline, and Congress, reinvigorated under the leadership of Sonia Gandhi, again won power in national elections. As a person of Italian origin, Mrs Gandhi declined to become prime minister in favour of Manmohan Singh, though she remains the power behind the throne. Under the new Congress, relations with Pakistan have improved greatly, and the Indian economy continues to prosper and expand.

Participation in the politics of the country is passionate and vocal

Gandhi

Born in 1869, son of the hereditary prime minister of the state of Kathiawar, Gujarat, Mohandas Karamchand Gandhi was married to Kasturba at the age of 13. He was sent to London to train as a barrister, but on his return, opted for a job in South Africa. His political career began in Durban when he was thrown out of a whites-only train carriage, and he started to work actively against the injustice of apartheid.

Returning to India in 1915, he was given the name Mahatma (Great Soul) by India's Nobel Laureate poet, Rabindranath Tagore, for his work in protecting the rights of poor farmers.

He quickly became a leader of the nationalist movement, espousing a philosophy of non-violent non-cooperation, *satyagraha*, based on a belief in self-reliance as a powerful force for change.

In 1920, he launched the first national campaign of civil disobedience. In 1921, he abandoned Western dress and adopted the plain white homespun

Mahatma ('a great soul') Gandhi became a revered figure in his home country, and a powerful influence for peace throughout the world

dhoti, both as a protest against foreign cloth imports, and in solidarity with the untouchables, whom he renamed the Harijan (Children of God). His dream was to eradicate the caste system and make independent India a truly classless society.

In 1930, he led a 200-mile march to the sea to make salt, and break the British government monopoly of this industry. In 1942, he launched the 'Quit India' campaign. Between negotiations with the government, he spent a number of years in jail, and embarked on several hunger strikes as a way of breaking political deadlock.

Gandhi was opposed to the Partition of India, and in 1947 once again went on hunger strike to try and stop the resulting animosity and massacre between Hindus and Muslims. Although he succeeded in halting communal riots at that time, the tragic culmination of his perceived support for Muslims was his assassination by a Hindu extremist in Delhi while on his way to evening prayer on 30 January 1948.

A totally extraordinary man, as politician, philosopher and social crusader, Gandhi is venerated as one of the greatest of all men, in India, and across the world.

Culture

The cities may have a large enough sprinkling of Western-style liberalism to confuse the visitor, but most of India lives by rules stretching back thousands of years. Regional variations in language, food, and customs are clearly visible, and whatever their beliefs, religion (*see pp20–23*) is more than a faith to all Indians; it is an inextricable part of the fabric of society.

A young village girl in festive finery

Caste

With Hinduism comes a rigid caste system that has also spread in a less determined form to India's other religions. Your caste has nothing to do with your financial standing or your education. The Brahmin peasant has a higher social standing than the Dalit (untouchable) doctor. A few daring souls may marry out of caste, and the Dalits do now have some constitutional rights, but the struggle to gain recognition on the social ladder is still a bitter one. Many are cynical and don't even try – they believe it is their *karma* (ordained fate), and hope for a better deal in the next life.

Lifestyle

There is a vast difference between rural and urban lifestyles. Indian men are hardworking, whether in the fields or in a white-collar job. The Indian male, however, is hugely pampered at home, and seldom shares in housework and child rearing. Leisure time is often spent in the company of other men, just as women feel more at ease with their own sex. Most marriages are still arranged, often between children barely into their

teens, and a dowry system flourishes despite efforts to eradicate it. Nevertheless, values are changing, especially among the educated in urban areas, as women increasingly assert their independence, and occupy influential positions on a par with men.

Increasingly, the young in urban families are opting for independent homes, although among the more traditional, the joint family system prevails, with elders given their rightful place in the family hierarchy in all rituals and customs.

Rajasthan

Rajasthan, for all its glories, is deeply conservative, and feudal values are well entrenched. The caste system itself is divided into hundreds of sub-castes.

The Rajputs (*see pp96–7*) still reign supreme. There is money among both the Rajputs and the mercantile Jains, but a vast number of people in the region still eke out a living. Conversely, some may seem poor when you see their humble village homes, but the women are draped in heavy silver jewellery, while a little boy guards the family herd of 30 camels. Among the former nomads, wealth is translated as movable personal goods, not land.

As a whole, the Rajasthanis are a handsome people, their classic features adorned by bright colours and rich ornamentation. The men are all too aware of their appearance, from the colour and ornate pattern of the turban, which proclaims the caste, occupation, and home area of the wearer, to the dashing curl of the moustache.

The women, too, look stunning, but in Rajasthan life can be brutal. As in medieval Europe, the chivalric Rajput warriors swore to love and protect their women. One way this was done was by adopting the Muslim custom of *purdah* (the veil), where life was confined to the *zenana* (women's quarters). In high society, this left the women with nothing to do; as the custom pervaded the lower social strata, women were almost entirely cut off from the outside world, even while they brought up several offspring, did all the cooking and cleaning, and helped with the farming – growing old before their time. Despite the stridency of some social activists, dowry deaths still occur, and *sati* (voluntary death by burning on a husband's funeral pyre, now illegal) shrines in Rajasthan attract hordes of women devotees who believe in their magical powers to cure infertility.

The news of the day is keenly read in English and the regional languages

Religion

Hinduism

To be Hindu describes your race, way of life, and whole being. A person is born a Hindu, there is no way to become, or stop being one, and the religion, which emerged in India in the second millennium BC with the Aryan people, is flexible enough to incorporate a multitude of beliefs.

As a Hindu, you live in a cycle of endless reincarnation (*samsara*), your deeds in this life determining your fate (*karma*) in the next. There are four aims: to acquire religious merit through right living (*dharma*), to make lawful money (*artha*), to satisfy desire (*kama*), and finally attain *moksha*, the end of the cycle of rebirth and merge with *Bhagvan*, the soul of the universe. *Puja* (ritual worship), cremation of the dead and adherence to the caste system are essential aspects of the faith.

There are rituals for every occasion, hundreds of festivals (*see pp24–5*), and pilgrimages are as popular as package tours. However, normal worship is essentially private.

People pop into the temple in passing to make an offering of flowers, fruit and money, and receive a blessing. Every household has a shrine, usually tended by the women. Even the morning wash is a prayer, as spiritual and physical purity are regarded as one.

The Gods

There is a huge pantheon of gods, goddesses, minor spirits and demons. However, most are actually different aspects or incarnations of the same few. At the top of the tree is the trinity – Brahma (the Creator), Shiva (the Destroyer) and Vishnu (the Preserver) – themselves probably different aspects of *Bhagvan*.

Although priests are called Brahmins, only one active temple to **Brahma** is left in India, at Pushkar, Rajasthan (*see p71*).

Vishnu is usually portrayed with a discus, conch shell, mace and lotus blossom. He rides the half-man, half-eagle **Garuda**. Of his ten incarnations, he has appeared nine times so far, when the earth was in great need. The most

HINDU RELIGIOUS TERMS

Ashram – place where spiritual community assembles

Avtar – incarnation of a god

Bhakti – act of devotion

Devi – Hindu goddess

Devata – minor Hindu god

Fakir – ascetic holy man

Garbhagriha – sanctuary at the heart of the temple, literally 'womb–house'

Guru – Hindu spiritual leader

Sadhu – wandering Hindu holy man

Shaiva – followers of Shiva

Shikhara – spire above the temple sanctuary

Swami – title given to an initiated monk

Vaishnava – followers of Vishnu

important are: the seventh, the hero **Rama**, whose epic adventures are told in the classical poem, the *Ramayana*; the eighth, **Krishna**, usually portrayed as a playful blue-faced child god with a flute (he is also the charioteer in the epic *Mahabharata* whose words are enshrined in the *Bhagwad Gita*); and the ninth, the **Buddha**, Prince Siddhartha Gautam.

Shiva is worshipped under many names. He is the Nataraja, Lord of the Dance, where he crushes evil under his foot; above all, he is the god of procreation, and his most common symbol is the phallic *lingam*. He is also shown with a third eye, sign of wisdom and power.

Of the goddesses, the most powerful is **Parvati**, wife of Shiva and sister of Vishnu. She is worshipped as the mother goddess, and as the terrifying **Durga** and Kali, goddess of destruction. **Lakshmi**, wife of **Vishnu**, is the goddess of wealth and good fortune, with several impressive temples built to honour her by grateful millionaires. Other more popular deities are the elephant-headed **Ganesh**, god of wisdom and

prosperity and the monkey god, **Hanuman**, who helped Rama on his quest for his wife, Sita. This martial god is also well versed in yoga and music, and Sanskrit grammar.

A wandering *sadhu* (holy man)

The ritual Muslim prayer is said on a special rug

Islam

Islam, founded in Mecca (now Saudi Arabia) by the Prophet Mohammed (c.AD 570–632) has a following of over 110 million Muslims in India, the second largest number after Indonesia. By the early 8th century, Islam controlled most of Arabia, and was spreading west into Europe and east towards India. Conquest of Delhi was finally achieved in 1192 by Mohammed Ghori (*see p9*).

The religion follows the teachings of the Prophet, revealed to him in a series of divine revelations from the one God, Allah, and set down in the Quran (Holy Book). Islam means 'submission to God'. The Five Pillars of Islam

(essential duties) include: prayer five times a day; the creed 'There is no God but Allah, and Mohammed is the messenger of God'; the annual month-long fast of Ramadan; alms-giving; and, if possible, the Haj – the pilgrimage to Mecca.

Muslims in India are both Shias and Sunnis. There are also many important shrines of Sufi saints in north India.

Jainism

An off-shoot of Hinduism, the Jain religion was founded in the 6th century BC by Vardhamana Jnatputra, who became known as Mahavira (great hero). He was the son of a wealthy family, and became a wandering ascetic. Jainism was originally purely monastic; a lay version of the religion (still considered inferior) wasn't conceived for another century. Mahavira said that true followers must renounce everything. After his death, there was a split between the *digambaras* ('sky-clad') who believed this meant rejecting all clothes, and the *shvetambaras* ('white-clad') who felt that a simple white robe could be allowed.

ISLAMIC RELIGIOUS TERMS

Allah – God

Dargah – shrine or tomb of a Muslim saint

Imam – person who leads the prayer

Imambara – man's tomb

Masjid – mosque (Jama Masjid means Friday Mosque)

Mihrab – niche in a mosque pointing the way to Mecca

Minbar – steps beside the *mihrab* pointing the way to heaven

Muezzin – man who calls the faithful to prayer

Minaret – tower from which the call to prayer is broadcast

Quran (Koran) – the holy book of Islam

Shia – hard-line sect which broke away soon after the Prophet's death, believing that the religion should be led by a direct descendant of the prophet

Sunni – the main body of Islam, which regards *imams* as teachers and accepts no absolute authority but God

Sufi – ascetic Muslim sect with mystic beliefs

Mahavira is believed to be the last of the 24 *tirthankaras* (prophets who help believers cross the bridge between the earthly and spiritual life). Images of the *tirthankaras* can be seen in all Jain temples. The universe is divided into four levels: the underworld, earth, celestial world and paradise. The aim in life is to detach yourself from the physical world through sacrifice, breaking the chains of the body to let the soul go free. It takes many rebirths to achieve this.

Monks and nuns travel for about eight months of the year, gathering to study and meditate during the monsoon. They renounce all possessions and live celibate lives. As a final renunciation of the flesh, the old are sometimes allowed to starve themselves to death on the road to paradise.

There are about 4 million Jains in India. Lay Jains must wait to become monks, and women to be reborn as men before they can come closer to liberation from existence in this universe. Jains are strict vegetarians; non-violence to any form of life is the essence of the religion.

Commerce and banking are regarded as non-violent occupations, which is why Jains are renowned traders, and the superb beauty of many Jain temples is the result of commercial profit.

Jain nuns lead an arduous life, based on total renunciation of worldly goods

Festivals

The Indian calendar is a continuous stream of festivities in celebration of every major and minor god, the seasons, and rites of passage. Most are basically private and never touch the visitor, but plenty are spectacular, filled with music and dance, fire crackers and processions. Added to these are the huge fairs or *melas*, cattle or camel markets. The dates follow the lunar calendar, which determines major Hindu as well as Muslim festivals.

A member of the camel brigade in festive finery

Republic Day
26 January, All India
India's most spectacular parade is along Rajpath in New Delhi. 'Floats' from all over India include highly decorated elephants, camels, horses, dancers and musicians, and a military procession. Tickets for seats are sold months ahead (*contact Thomas Cook, p185*).

Desert Festival
February, Jaisalmer
Totally for tourists, the Jaisalmer Desert Festival is noisy and colourful, with camel races, a Mr Desert 'beauty' pageant, and a best moustache competition. There is also a Bikaner Desert Festival.

Holi
March, North India
The traditional Hindu festival of colour celebrates the end of winter, the destruction of the demon Holika. People mark the day by bombarding each other with coloured water, dye, or watery clay and cattle dung, and by drinking opium-based *bhang*. In the city of

Jaipur, there is a splendid Elephant Festival, with elephant polo played at Chaugan Stadium.

Gangaur
March/April, Jaipur
Primarily a women's festival, celebrating married bliss and fertility. Images of Shiva and his consort Parvati are decorated and carried in procession, with dancing and music.

Teej
August, Jaipur
Celebrating the reunion of Shiva and Parvati, and the onset of the monsoon, women dress up and take turns on brightly decorated swings. There are processions with idols, elephants, traditional songs and dance.

Dussehra
September/October, All India
A popular ten-day festival, celebrating the victory of the goddess Durga over the demon, Mahishasura and Rama over the demon king, Ravana. People perform the *Ram Lila* (story of the

Ramayana), and burn effigies of the demons on the tenth day, amidst the booming sound of fire crackers. This is traditionally also the start of the military campaigning season, marked by a magnificent procession in Jaipur.

Diwali
October/November, All India
The Festival of Lights is the biggest event of the Hindu calendar, when every building is lit up by candles, oil lamps, and even fairy lights, to light Rama's path on his journey home after the rescue of Sita. The accompanying sound of fire crackers fills the night air. It is also the Hindu New Year. People traditionally give each other sweets, and spring-clean their houses in honour of the fastidious goddess of wealth, Lakshmi.

Pushkar Mela
November, Pushkar
Over the full moon or Kartik Poornima, Hindu pilgrims come in thousands to bathe in the sacred lake. Alongside is India's largest cattle, camel and horse fair. Pushkar now attracts some 50,000 foreign tourists a year, and huge tented villages and entertainment programmes are laid on to keep them amused.
The Rajasthan Tourism Development Corporation sets up tented villages at the most entertaining festival sites. Book through any RTDC office (see p186).

Businessmen wrap their new account books in red cloth for the Diwali festival

Impressions

'This is indeed India! The land of dreams and romance, of fabulous wealth and fabulous poverty, of splendour and rags, of palaces and hovels, of famine and pestilence, of genii and giants and Aladdin lamps . . . the one land that all men desire to see, and having once seen, by even a glimpse, would not give that glimpse for the shows of all the rest of the globe combined.'

MARK TWAIN, *More Tramps Abroad*, 1897

A villager carrying water from a public supply

GETTING AROUND

Traffic on Indian roads is made up of an unbelievable variety of road users, from buses to bullock carts. Most middle-class Indians own either cars or two-wheel motor vehicles. There is also a busy and affordable public transport system, from railways, to buses and taxis, and the ubiquitous three-wheel auto-rickshaw (tricycle with an out-board motor and a covering).

Cars and taxis

It is rarely worth hiring a private car in the main cities as there are numerous taxis, most of which have a fixed rate for the full day. Small towns have few if any taxis, but there are private car agencies who hire out on a day to day basis. For out of town touring by car, all the international car hire companies have offices in the major cities. They will probably insist on you having a driver, but wages are cheap, and you save the cost of insurance, so it can be financially worthwhile, as well as much less stressful. Consider going one stage further; book through a travel agent, and use a driver/guide who will speak better English, act as a personal courier and also iron out any problems you face en route. It costs little more.

Outboards, horses and pedal power

Auto-rickshaws are the mainstay of urban transport in India, zipping through the traffic at exhaust pipe level. Some people loathe them, others become addicted. Some towns also have slightly larger autos which take up to ten people, and act as shared taxis. Cycle rickshaws are less common these days, but do still exist. Try one for the experience, but they are really only suitable for short distances, and can be very alarming in heavy traffic. In a very few country towns you will meet *tongas*, drawn by ageing skeletal nags.

Buses

There are plenty of buses, almost all very uncomfortable and overcrowded. Luxury long-distance coaches come with air-conditioning and lace curtains, but the videos and Hindi pop music inside can wear you down. Before you book,

Dare-devil auto-rickshaws are everywhere

consider that some inter-city journeys last over ten hours. Every town has a central bus station. They are usually chaotic, with no recognisable system of platforms or bays. Just keep asking everyone you meet if you are in the right place; sooner or later, you will be.

Local services can be harder to find as there is never a timetable or list of routes. However, auto-rickshaws are cheap enough to justify using them.

For planes, see p178; for trains, see below.

Indian railways

Founded in 1853, one of the earliest and busiest networks in the world (and the world's largest employer, with about 1.8 million employees), Indian Railways carries over 4,500 million passengers a year. A massive upgrading programme has been converting all the tracks in Rajasthan to broad gauge, bringing in fast, modern capabilities. A sad by-product has been the virtual demise of steam in place of diesel. Nevertheless, train travel is an experience not to be missed. The very few superfast, air-conditioned, first-class carriages are similar to European second class.

The cycle rickshaw is still popular in the older parts of Delhi

Country buses carry three times the legal number of passengers

Normal first class is much scruffier, while second class often has hard benches and heaving heaps of bodies. The extraordinarily grand stations (imperial Indian, by way of Waterloo) are teeming with life from beggars to businessmen. Luggage from fancy leather suitcases to cloth bundles clutters the platforms.

Indrail passes
Available only abroad or in selected major railway stations, these rail passes, bought in foreign currency, are usually more expensive than booking individual tickets, but you will get preferential treatment and save a lot of time and hassle. The recommended first-class pass includes II AC (air-conditioned

second class, but better than fan-cooled first class). There are half-day to 90-day versions, the most useful being:
7 days (US $135)
15 days (US $185)
21 days (US $198)
30 days (US $248)
Sleepers for night travel are free of charge.

Choosing your train
Outlying places may have only one or two trains a day. Other routes have a great many, but the travelling time can vary enormously (for example, from under two hours to four and a half hours between Delhi and Agra), depending on the type of train. Mail trains and passenger trains are slowest express trains faster and

FARE PRICE

Taxis and autos in Delhi all have meters; many work and many do not. Meters can never be upgraded fast enough to keep up with inflation, so the municipality hands out cards with the new prices from time to time. Be sure to check before you start a journey, and if necessary fix the fare in advance, especially in Agra and Rajasthan. This could involve some serious haggling. Ask someone friendly roughly how long your journey is and what the fare should be before you start. If you are in the wrong place, for example, the gateway of a 5-star hotel, or the front of the railway station, expect the first price to be several times higher than normal. As a rule of thumb elsewhere, look to drop the price by half to two-thirds. If you are doing a lot of running around, it is well worth hiring a vehicle (they always come with a driver) or an auto for a half or whole day.

superfast express really fast. All services have numbers and names. Many of the most convenient for longer distances are overnight, or leave at the crack of dawn.

Reservations

All major stations have a tourist booking office or window. For overnight journeys, reserve a berth as far ahead as possible, even if you have a pass. Fill in a form with the name and number of the train and your personal details. If you get stuck on a stand-by list, ask about the tourist quota – a few seats may still be available.

The Palace on Wheels

The ultimate train trip, this luxury seven-day train cruise whistles round Rajasthan for around US $395 per person per day. The original train used vintage carriages; the new version is an excellent replica with air conditioning, proper plumbing and royal service.

Mobile stall at a railway station

Further Information

SD Enterprises Ltd (Indian Railways agents), 103 Wembley Park Drive, Wembley, Middlesex HA9 8HG. *Tel: (020) 8903 3411; Fax: (020) 8903 0392.*
Hariworld Travels Inc (Indian Railways agents), 25 W 45th St #1003, New York, NY 10036. *Tel: (212) 997 3000; Fax: (212) 997 3320; hari-world@hari-world.com*

Trains are a stress-free way to cover long distances

Above: Four-footed transport is still alive and kicking
Below: Licensed porters are recognisable by their usually faded red jackets and turbans

International Tourist Bureau, New Delhi Railway Station Building, 1st floor, Chelmsford Rd, New Delhi.
Tel: (011) 340 5156/334 6804;
Fax: (011) 334 3050.
Palace on Wheels, Rajasthan Tourism Development Corporation Central Reservation Offices (*see p186*).

The bi-monthly *Thomas Cook Overseas Timetable* gives details of rail, bus and shipping services worldwide. Available in the UK from some stations, any branch of Thomas Cook, or tel: (01733) 416477.

LIVING WITH INDIA
Culture shock

Among the poorer countries of the world, India has all the attendant social ills to shock a first-time visitor. Dust, disease and poverty are inevitable aspects of a developing nation that is

A holy man in front of Agra Fort

beggar, a little bribe to smooth the path, or something expected of you, as a rich foreigner, for no reason at all. It is a word that will follow you wherever you go. You will have to deal with would-be guides, drivers, salesmen and beggars. You cannot give to them all, and should not give to some. Many are genuinely needy, but there are also organised begging rings, and children are often exploited to extract money from bleeding-heart foreigners. You are likely to be swamped by people if you are seen to be handing out cash – it may be a better idea to give a decent donation to a charity instead.

overrun by a burgeoning population. In India, bureaucratic hurdles can seem impassable. Curious crowds stare and giggle. You can hide briefly inside the Westernised hotels, but that just means you never acclimatise and are shocked anew each time you step out.

Don't expect to have a relaxing holiday. Accept the fact that you may well spend much of your time in a state of bewildered chaos, and you will probably only understand what you experienced about six months after you arrive home, exhausted, but considerably richer in experience.

Treat the queues, the crowds and the flies as part of the adventure, and every so often treat your sanity to a little luxury – a hot bath, a swim or a cool gin-and-tonic.

Baksheesh and beggars
Baksheesh can be a tip, a donation to a

Shoes left by the temple door

A children's brigade clamouring for *baksheesh*

Body language

Always greet people politely, with a smile. Men can shake hands, but women should fold their hands in a *namaste* (as in prayer). Men and women never touch in public, and this extends to your own spouse. Only Westernised men will shake hands with a woman. Never use your left hand for eating, or for giving anything to someone else (the left hand is kept for ablutions).

Religious etiquette

Although there are many religions and sects, the basic rules of etiquette in places of worship are the same. Always dress modestly – no shorts and no bare shoulders, and cover your head when inside. Always take off your shoes; the shoeminder by the door will expect a tip of a few rupees. Never take leather into a Jain temple or Hindu temple. A few temples may bar non-Hindus from the inner sanctum, but most will encourage you to take part in any celebration and show you the ropes. Try to avoid mosques at Friday lunchtime, but you will be welcome at all other times.

Women travellers

Small-town Indians may find you bizarre, but travelling on your own is not a problem if you exercise caution. You will get requests for everything, from a quick fling to marriage, but the people are usually polite, and a firm 'no' works wonders. Personal questions stem from curiosity. Try not to dress in clothes which could be considered provocative; many women in Rajasthan still live in *purdah*. Most Indian women do not drink or smoke.

Photography

Take far more film than you would ever expect to want, and you will probably still end up needing more. It is possible to buy film in most tourist areas, but the range on offer is limited, and you should always check the sell-by date. The light is good, if too harsh at midday, so take mainly slow film, with some faster ISOs for interiors and evenings. Large cities all have excellent developing and printing shops.

You are allowed to take photos inside many monuments, museums and temples, but you will usually need to buy an additional photo ticket or pay a donation to a nearby monk (who will also pose, if the price is right). If you use a tripod, you will probably be classified as professional, and the cost goes up dramatically. Video cameras are a real nuisance, as they have to be declared on entry. They are forbidden in many places, and in others the price for using them is very high. Photography of any military installation (including bridges) or soldiers is forbidden. People usually turn a blind eye at railway stations, but you should ask the superintendent for permission, or apply for a permit from the Director of Public Relations, Railway Board, Rail Bhavan, New Delhi 110 001 (*tel: (011) 338 1332*).

Some beggars, snake charmers and opportunists will ask for money; set a rate before you start clicking. However, most Indians, apart from women in *purdah*, love being photographed, and huge crowds will line up as soon as they spot the camera. You will also find Indian tourists asking to take pictures of you – it seems only fair to let them!

Keen photographers in Bharatpur sanctuary

Delhi

Delhi has a pedigree stretching back at least 4,500 years, with around 20,000 known ruins, and 1,300 listed monuments. Moreover, for most of its life, it has been an imperial capital, and the home of kings. Today, it is the capital of a united India, and the third largest city on the subcontinent after Mumbai (Bombay) and Kolkata (Calcutta), with a population of almost 14 million, that is constantly growing.

'[Delhi] is the most uncertain-minded of cities in the world. It is like a fidgety girl who will first sit here, and there, then somewhere else, and fifty square miles of ground and twenty thousand ruins tell where it has rested.'
JOHN FOSTER FRASER, *Round the World on a Wheel*, 1899

A huge north–south sprawl along the banks of the Yamuna River, the city has two distinct and very different centres. To the south are the wide tree-lined boulevards and colonnaded mansions of British-built New Delhi, the official seat of government. To the north, Mughal Old Delhi (once known as Shahjahanabad) is an overcrowded frenzy of narrow winding streets and alleys. Beyond, in every direction, spread suburbs and housing colonies, blocks of flats and, carefully away from the centre, an oozing mass of shanty towns and grubby slums.

When most people arrive, they are disappointed by how tatty the city centre seems. A few weeks later, the lucky ones look beyond the peeling paint and faded posters and suddenly see a different city glowing with wealth and modernity – by Indian standards. Both impressions are right. Like the rest of India, Delhi has a multiple personality. It isn't instantly and obviously beautiful. The constant press of people can be irritating; there is noise and dust, although efforts at curbing vehicular emissions have eased levels of pollution. Given time, you will begin to feel the sheer weight of history, the grace and good nature, and the constant buzz of excitement that makes this one of the great cities of the world.

Connaught Place, at the centre of New Delhi

Delhi City

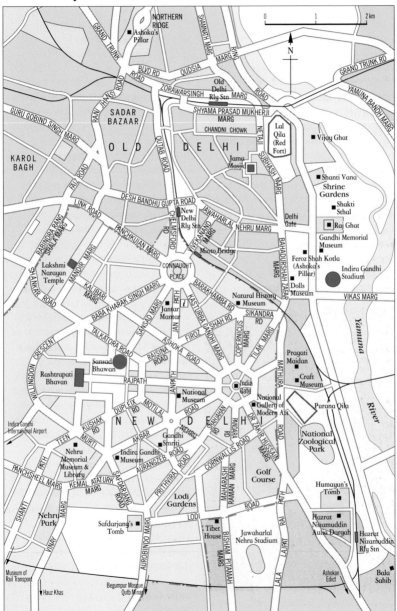

Delhi City map labels:

NORTHERN RIDGE
Ashoka's Pillar
GRAND TRUNK ROAD
SHAMNATH MARG
BLVD RD
QUDSIA MARG
ZORAWARSINGH
RING ROAD
GRAND TRUNK RD
YAMUNA BANDH MARG
Old Delhi Rly Stn
RANI JHANSI ROAD
GURU GOBIND SINGH MARG
SADAR BAZAAR
SHYAMA PRASAD MUKHERJI MARG
CHANDNI CHOWK
NETAJI
Lal Qila (Red Fort)
Vijay Ghat
KAROL BAGH
O L D   D E L H I
QUTAB ROAD
Jama Masjid
SUBHASH MARG
Shanti Vana
Shrine Gardens
FAIZ ROAD
LINK ROAD
DESH BANDHU GUPTA ROAD
Shakti Sthal
PANCHKUIAN MARG
CHELMSFORD RD
New Delhi Rly Stn
JAWAHARLAL NEHRU MARG
VIVEKANAND MARG
Delhi Gate
Raj Ghat
BAHADURSHAH ZAFAR MARG
Gandhi Memorial Museum
RABINDRA RANG SHALA MARG
MANDIR MARG
Minto Bridge
CONNAUGHT PLACE
Feroz Shah Kotla (Ashoka's Pillar)
Indira Gandhi Stadium
SHANKAR ROAD
Lakshmi Narayan Temple
KALIBARI MARG
BABA KHARAK SINGH MARG
BARAKHAMBA RD
Dolls Museum
VIKAS MARG
Natural History Museum
i
SANSAD MARG
JAN PATH
KASTURBA GANDHI MARG
FIROZ SHAH RD
SIKANDRA RD
COPERNICUS MARG
Jantar Mantar
TALKATORA ROAD
ASHOKA ROAD
TILAK MARG
MATHURA ROAD
Pragati Maidan
WILLINGDON CRESCENT
RAISINA ROAD
RAJPATH
Sansad Bhawan
Craft Museum
Rashtrapati Bhawan
Purana Qila
JANPATH
National Museum
India Gate
National Gallery of Modern Art
National Zoological Park
Yamuna River
Indira Gandhi International Airport
DUPLEIX RD
MOTILAL
KUSHAK RD
N E W   •   D E L H I
NEHRU
DR ZAKIR HUSSAIN MARG
TEEN MURTI
AKBAR ROAD
Gandhi Smriti
SHAHJAHAN RD
RAJENDRA
PANCHSHEEL MARG
Nehru Memorial Museum & Library
Indira Gandhi Museum
AURANGZEB ROAD
CORNWALLIS ROAD
MAHARASHI RAMAN MARG
Golf Course
Humayun's Tomb
KEMAL ATATURK MARG
SAFDARJANG ROAD
PRITHVIRAJ ROAD
Lodi Gardens
Hazrat Nizamuddin Aulia Dargah
Hazrat Nizamuddin Rly Stn
SHANTI PATH
VINAY MARG
Nehru Park
Safdarjang's Tomb
AUROBINDO MARG
LODI ROAD
Tibet House
BISHAM PITAMAH MARG
Jawaharlal Nehru Stadium
LALA LAJPAT RAI PATH
Bala Sahib
Museum of Rail Transport
Begumpur Mosque
Qutb Minar
Hauz Khas
Ashokan Edict

0   1   2 km

N

Baha'i House of Worship

This enormous lotus blossom of white concrete and marble, designed by an Iranian architect, was completed in 1986. Its nine sides and nine reflective pools symbolise comprehensiveness, oneness and unity, while the lotus is a traditional Indian symbol of purity and holiness. Baha'i communities are spread all over India, dedicated to promoting worldwide peace and unity.

Bahapur, Kalkaji, South Delhi. Tel: (011) 2644 4029. Open: Apr–Sep, Tue–Sun 9am–7pm; Oct–Mar 9.30am–5.30pm. Free admission.

Connaught Place

See p47.

Nizamuddin Aulia Complex

One of the holiest Islamic sites in India, this is the *dargah* (shrine) of the saint

The onion domes of the Jama Masjid, Old Delhi

Nizamuddin Aulia (1236–1325) of the Chishti sect of Sufis. During a major quarrel with the Tughlaq king, Ghiyasuddin, he prophesied that Ghiyasuddin's new city of Tughlaqabad would become a home for sheep, and that the king wouldn't live to see Delhi again. Both prophesies came true. The existing domed tomb was built in 1526 to replace the older one. *Qawwalis* (mystical poems) are sung at about 7pm every evening, and all night during the twice-yearly Urs fairs which celebrate the anniversaries of Sufi saints.

Diagonally opposite Humayun's tomb, off Mathura Rd. Free admission.

Humayun's Tomb

Emperor Humayun died in 1556, tripping down the stairs of the Purana Qila on his way to prayer. His magnificent mausoleum, completed in 1573 by his senior widow, is the first of the great Mughal buildings in India, a huge octagonal building of red sandstone, inlaid with white and black marble, resting upon an arcaded plinth, and topped by a bulbous 42.5m-high double dome. Set four-square in walled gardens divided by water channels (the *charbagh*), it created the pattern followed by generations of classic Islamic garden tombs, including the Taj Mahal. Most of the tombs are royal, but the finest belong to the king's barber and bangle-maker.

Off Mathura Rd, near Nizamuddin Station. Open: sunrise–sunset. Admission & photo charge.

India Gate

See p46.

Astronomical wonder, Jantar Mantar, New Delhi

Jantar Mantar

One of five observatories built by Jaipur's astronomer king, Jai Singh II, in 1724, this may look like a playground, but is in fact a complex system for measuring time (accurate to half a second), the seasons, the movements of celestial bodies and even the signs of the zodiac. (*See also pp98–9.*)
Sansad Marg (no telephone). Open: daily sunrise–sunset. Admission charge.

Lakshmi Narayan Temple

A large, somewhat gaudy temple, built in 1938 by the industrialist Birla family, and dedicated to the goddess of wealth. It is a typical example of modern temple architecture.
Mandir Marg. Free admission.

Jama Masjid (Friday Mosque)

Built between 1650 and 1656 by Emperor Shah Jahan, this is the largest and most splendid mosque in India, capable of holding 25,000 people. Constructed from red sandstone, marble and black onyx, it has two minarets, three domes and three pulpits so that three *imams* (priests) can pray simultaneously to the immense crowds. Perched on a high plinth, it was originally and aptly named the Masjid -i-Jahan Nama (Mosque with a View of the World). A small museum in the cloisters holds holy relics, including a hair from Prophet Mohammed's beard, his sandals and a footprint set in stone.
Opposite the Red Fort, Netaji Subhash Marg. Tel: (011) 2326 8344. Open: daily sunrise–noon; 1.45pm until 20 minutes before afternoon prayer call; after prayers until 20 minutes before sunset. Admission & photo charge.

The Lakshmi Narayan Temple in New Delhi is a 20th-century construction that follows the traditional style of temple architecture

Lal Qila (Red Fort)

When Shah Jahan moved his capital to Delhi, he built a magnificent palace, decorated it with marble and precious stones, tapestries and carpets, created formal gardens set with gushing fountains, and called it the *Qila-e-Mubarak* (Fortunate Citadel). Work began in 1638, took nearly ten years, and cost almost Rs 90 million. Its current prosaic title is something of a let-down, matched by its sorry state after earthquakes, invasions, attacks and fires. Conservation activity has only recently begun.

After the 1857 Mutiny, the last Mughal emperor was tried here, and about two-thirds of its buildings demolished to make way for army barracks, and much of the rest stripped out by the British. At midnight on 14 August 1947, the new flag was raised here to mark the birth of India's independence.

The walls

The roughly octagonal red sandstone walls measure 2.4km all round, 18m to 33m high, and are surrounded by a 9m-deep moat, fed by the Yamuna River (now almost dry). Of the five gates, only the **Lahore Gate** remains in use, its triumphal effect blocked by a massive barbican built by Emperor Aurangzeb. Inside, the **Chatta Chowk** (covered market) was built to sell luxury goods to the courtiers. It now sells souvenirs.

Naubat or Naqqar Khana (Drum House)

Just inside the entrance, this three-storey building was used for music and fanfares and as the visitors' elephant park. Two emperors, Jahandar Shah (1712–13) and Farrukhsiyar (1713–19) were murdered here. The upper storeys house a small **War Memorial Museum**.

Diwan-i-Aam (Hall of Public Audience)

Directly ahead, the emperor would hold court each morning in this space, his throne perched on the massive platform, with the *wazir* (prime minister) sitting on the bench in front. Curtains and carpets decorated the pavilion, which at that time would have been plastered and gilded. Behind the throne is an intricate marble panel, created by the Florentine jeweller, Austin de Bordeaux.

Private quarters

The inner palace consists of a string of small pavilions along the river wall. On the far left, the delicately carved marble **Moti Masjid** (Pearl Mosque) was built by Aurangzeb in 1659. A canopy shaded the courtyard in which a fountain ran hot and cold water. Behind it is the **Hammam**, or royal Bath House.

To the right of this, the **Diwan-i-Khas** (Hall of Private Audience) was the real centre of government, and home of the Peacock Throne of solid gold decorated with jewelled peacocks, stolen by Nadir Shah in 1739 and taken to Tehran.

At the centre of the complex, the **Khas Mahal** (Private Palace) housed the emperor's own quarters. The emperor would wave to his subjects from the balcony behind this building every morning and evening. The harem buildings began with the **Rang Mahal** (known as the House of Colour or House of Mirrors for its once brilliant decoration). The whole area was cooled by underfloor streams, pools and fountains called the **Nahr-i-Bihisht** (Stream of Paradise). On the far right, the marble Mumtaz Mahal now houses the **Museum of Archaeology**.

Off Netaji Subhash Marg, Old Delhi. Tel: (011) 2326 7961/2327 3703. Open: daily 9am–5pm; museums 10am–5pm (closed Fri). Admission charge (free on Fri). Son et Lumière, see p159.

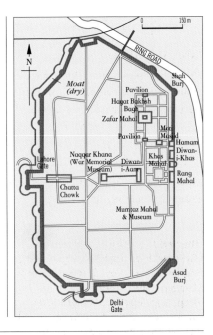

The Lahore Gate is now the only entrance to Shah Jahan's massive Red Fort

There is a fight for supremacy on the road involving one brightly painted lorry belching black smoke, three battered buses, with people clinging to windows and bumpers like barnacles, numerous snarling black and yellow auto-rickshaws, a camel-cart laden with fridges, a couple of shiny Ambassador cars and a family of five on a motor-scooter. The few spaces between are taken up by a positive regiment of young men on elderly black bicycles,

and coming up from behind is an elephant. The lorry sports a sign that says 'Horn, please' – everybody else is only too eager to oblige, and the noise level is fantastic. Slap bang in the middle

of the road, several creamy-white cows with painted horns have sat down to chew the cud and watch the traffic swirl around them. Half-a-dozen ragged children, cripples and lepers dodge through the mayhem, thrusting grubby hands into any open window. 'Rupee, just one rupee, my mother is ill, my father is ill…' On a tiny patch of open ground a shanty town of cardboard and corrugated iron has sprung up, puffing little gasps of smoke from a dozen tiny bonfires. Pride of place, in the shade of the trees, goes to the drivers who live and sleep in their cycle rickshaws. Beside them, a barber has set up shop with a chair, a pair of scissors and a bucket of water, and an old woman with a hand cart is selling peeled cucumbers and roast corn.

Nearby, a row of narrow, open-fronted shops is doing brisk business in anything from saucepans to Pepsi, blankets to statues of Ganesh. The older men sit cross-legged and calm, while milling crowds of young men in shiny nylon shirts and plastic thongs hang around waiting for something to happen. You, the hapless visitor, are not only a source of revenue, but also the entertainment.

India's streets are a whole world in themselves; people live, sleep, wash, eat, shop, chat and run their businesses in a haze of carbon monoxide and an ear-splitting cacophony of noise

MUSEUMS
Crafts Museum

A not-to-be-missed collection of crafts from across India, from toys to shrines, roof tiles to fishing traps, jewellery to puppets. Highlights include textiles, a reconstructed *haveli* and the Keralan Bhuta wood carvings. Outside, craftspeople demonstrate their skills and sell their wares in a reconstructed village square, while folk dancers perform.

Pragati Maidan, Bhairon Rd.
Tel: (011) 2331 7641. Open: Oct–Jun, Tue–Sun 10am–5pm. The crafts shop on site is open all year round at these hours. Free admission.

Memorial statue to Mahatma Gandhi

Gandhi Memorial Museums

These three museums celebrate the Mahatma (*see pp16–17*). The **Gandhi Darshan** displays his life, work and philosophy in photographs and paintings. The **Gandhi Smarak Sangrahalaya** is a more intimate collection of personal possessions. The colonial-style **Gandhi Smriti** was Gandhi's Delhi base. He was assassinated here in 1948. Inside is a fascinating display of his life; outside, a memorial stands in beautiful gardens.

Gandhi Darshan (tel: (011) 2335 9865) and Gandhi Smarak Sangrahalaya (tel: (011) 2331 0168) (closed Thur) are both opposite Raj Ghat. Open: Tue–Sun 9.30am–5pm. Films in English shown daily, 10am–5pm. Free admission. Gandhi Smriti, 5 Tees January Marg. Tel: (011) 2301 2843. Open: Tue–Sun 9am–5.30pm. Admission charge.

Indira Gandhi Museum

This simple house where Prime Minister Indira Gandhi and her family lived was converted to a museum after her death. Photographs, documents, and awards made to her and son Rajiv Gandhi, who succeeded her as prime minister, comprise the collection. It also includes Indira's wedding sari and the one worn by her when she was fatally shot by her own guard members in the grounds in 1984, as well as the trainers Rajiv was wearing when he was assassinated by a 'human bomb' in Madras in 1991.

1 Safdarjang Rd. Tel: (011) 2301 0094. Open: Tue–Sun 9.30am–5pm. Free admission.

Museum of Rail Transport

Contained within this museum is everything you would ever want to know about Indian railways, with photographs, models, 42 vintage locomotives, including the *Fairy Queen,* the oldest working engine in the world (built in 1855), 26 carriages, one used by the Prince of Wales in 1876 and a mini-train for children. Look for the elephant that tangled with a train (and nearly won), and the complaint from a man caught with his *dhoti* down.
Chanakyapuri. Tel: (011) 2688 0804. Open: Oct–Mar, Tue–Sun 9.30am–5.30pm; Apr–Sep 9.30am–7.30pm. Closed for lunch 12.30–1.30pm. Admission & photo charge. A film (English) is shown at 11am & 3pm.

National Gallery of Modern Art

In this fine collection of mainly post-1930s Indian art, housed in the former palace of the Maharaja of Jaipur, Indian subjects are treated with a rare freedom of expression. Among its highlights are the works of Amrita Shergill, and the Nobel Laureate poet, Rabindranath Tagore. There is also a sculpture garden in the grounds.
Jaipur House, India Gate. Tel: (011) 2338 2835. Open: Tue–Sun 10am–5pm. Free admission.

Nehru Memorial Museum and Planetarium

This 1930s mansion was the official residence of Prime Minister Jawaharlal Nehru (*see p14*). Inside, photos and newspapers tell the story of Nehru, from child to elder statesman. Several rooms are as he left them. Additions include a

Sculpture garden at the Gallery of Modern Art

planetarium and an excellent library for research scholars.
Teen Murti Bhavan. Tel: (011) 2301 6734. Open: Tue–Sun 9.30am–5pm. Planetarium (tel: (011) 2301 4504) open: 9am–4pm; audio visual in English at 11am & 3pm. Free admission.

Minor Museums
For a full list of other museums, see *Delhi Diary (p158)*. More interesting are:
National Philatelic Museum (*see p47*).
National Police Museum Lodi Rd. *Open: Mon–Fri 10am–5.50pm. Free admission.*
National Science Centre Museum Pragati Maidan. *Open: Tue–Sun 10am–6pm.*
Natural History Museum (*see p47*).
Tibet House Museum 1 Institutional Area, Lodi Rd. *Open: Mon–Fri 11am–6pm.*

Shankar's International Dolls Museum

Over 6,000 dolls from all over the world, collected by journalist and cartoonist, K Shankar Pillai, are housed here. Among the finest are those clothed in traditional Indian regional costumes.

Nehru House, Bahadurshah Zafar Marg. Tel: (011) 2331 6970. Open: Tue–Sun 10am–6pm. Admission charge.

National Museum

Allow a day to do real justice to India's national collection which includes a magnificent array of temple statuary, a wide range of costumes and textiles, miniature art, musical instruments, folk art, an archaeological collection (including Harappan and Gupta exhibits), a heavily guarded jewellery gallery and much, much more.

Janpath, just off Rajpath. Tel: (011) 2301 9272. Open: Tue–Sun 10am–5pm. Regular film shows and guided tours. Admission & photo charge.

Qutb Minar complex

Its magnificent early Islamic buildings dominate the site of the Rajput city of Dhilli/Lal Kot (*see p50*), better known now as Mehrauli.

Qutb Minar

This superb, 72-m high tower (1193–1230) served a dual purpose, as a resplendent minaret, and a very visible reminder of the area's new Islamic rulers. The original four-tier sandstone tower was built by Qutbuddin Aibak and Shamsuddin Iltutmish (1211–36). After the top storey was damaged by lightning in 1368, Feroz Shah Tughlaq repaired it, adding two storeys of Rajasthani marble and sandstone. Today, the tower is five storeys high, and slightly out of alignment after British repairs. With its adroit use of stone, Quranic engravings, and imaginative detail in each of the different tiers, it is one of the tallest and most beautiful minarets ever conceived. The **Alai Minar,** a second, bigger tower opposite, was begun by Alauddin Khalji (1296–1316) but never completed.

Quwwat ul-Islam Masjid (Might of Islam Mosque)

No fewer than the remains

THE IRON PILLAR

Brought here by one of the 10th- to 12th-century Tomar kings, the iron pillar is 7.2m high, weighs six tons, is made of 99.97 per cent pure iron, and has confounded scientists because it has never rusted. A Sanskrit inscription at the base shows it to be a 4th-century standard to the god Vishnu in memory of King Chandragupta II (375–413). Local lore promises good fortune to those who can encircle it backwards with both their hands touching, but sadly, the pillar is now fenced off and inaccessible.

of 27 Hindu and Jain temples, destroyed by Qutbuddin Aibak, were reused within this stunning mosque, the earliest extant in India (1192–8). Later additions were made by two successors, Shamsuddin Iltutmish, and then by Alauddin Khalji, resulting in a spectacular confection of seven types of stone, decorated with Quranic script. Standing in the courtyard is an iron pillar (*see box*), a remarkable testimony to early Indian metallurgical science.

Other sights

Behind the Qutb Minar is a purely Islamic monumental gateway, the **Alai Darwaza** (1311). Next to it is the small, attractive **tomb** of the early 16th-century Islamic saint, Imam Zamin. Behind the mosque are the remains of the **theological college**, and the **tombs of Alauddin Khalji** and **Shamsuddin Iltutmish**. The latter is particularly beautiful, every inch of the exterior carved with Quranic script. *The Qutb Minar complex is 15km south of Connaught Place off Aurobindo Marg. Open: sunrise–sunset. The tower itself is now closed to the public for safety reasons. Admission charge.*

Raj Ghat

The focal point of this serene park is the moving memorial in the form of a simple square platform in black marble which marks the site of Mahatma Gandhi's cremation. Northwards, along the old course of the Yamuna River, other memorials mark the cremation grounds of Jawaharlal Nehru (1964), Lal Bahadur Shastri (prime minister after Nehru, 1965), Indira Gandhi (1984) and Rajiv Gandhi (1991). *South of the Red Fort. Open: Apr–Sept, daily 5am–8pm; Oct–Mar 5.30am–7.30pm. Free admission.*

Rajpath

See p46.

Safdarjang's tomb

Safdarjang was the title given to the viceroy of Oudh and powerful prime minister to Emperor Muhammed Shah (1719–48). His mausoleum was built by his son in 1754 of highly decorated sandstone, with a central dome – the last of the classic Islamic garden tombs. *Safdarjang Rd. Open: sunrise–sunset. Admission & photo charge.*

The soaring Qutb Minar is a stunning monument to spiritual glory and earthly power

Tour: New Delhi

New Delhi was built between 1913 and 1931, a planned city of gracious boulevards and elegant colonial architecture, the work of Sir Edwin Landseer Lutyens and Herbert Baker. Hire an auto-rickshaw or taxi.

Allow two hours minimum; a whole day if you plan to sightsee and shop.

India Gate stands at the end of Rajpath boulevard

Start at India Gate.

1 India Gate

This 42-m triumphal arch is India's main war memorial, carved with the names of some 85,000 Indian soldiers killed during World War I in Europe and the Middle East, and during the Afghan Wars of the same time. Under the arch is an eternal flame, a memorial to soldiers who died during the brief 1971 war with Pakistan.

The cupola behind once housed a statue of King George V. Removed at Independence, and now lying forgotten at Coronation Park, it was to be replaced with a statue of Gandhi, but this has not yet been done.

In the surrounding circle of former princely palaces, Jaipur House is home to the National Gallery of Modern Art (*see p43*), and Bikaner House has the offices of Rajasthan Tourism.
Set off along Rajpath.

2 Rajpath

This ceremonial boulevard really comes into its own for the annual Republic Day parade on 26 January when the president of India takes the salute at a spectacular display by the armed forces.

Schoolchildren and imaginative floats depicting the states of India add to the colour and celebration.
Continue up Rajpath. Halfway up, the road is intersected by Janpath. Just to the left is the National Museum (see p44).

3 Rashtrapati Bhavan and Secretariat Buildings

At the far end of Rajpath, three vast imperial buildings squat on Raisina Hill. To either side, Herbert Baker's Secretariat buildings (North Block and South Block) house the Ministries of Finance and Foreign Affairs. At the back, Lutyens' magnificent Rashtrapati Bhavan, built as the Viceroy's house, is now the official residence of the Indian president. Larger than Versailles, with 340 rooms, it once had a staff of 2,000. The layout of the Secretariat buildings, which blocks views of the classical mansion, caused a two-year feud between the two architects.
Turn right along Sansad Marg, past a large circular colonnaded building. This is the Sansad Bhavan (Houses of Parliament). At the junction with Ashoka Rd is the important, but less than riveting, National Philatelic Museum. Further on is Maharaja Jai Singh's

outdoor observatory, the Jantar Mantar (see p37).

4 Connaught Place

The heart of Lutyens' new city and the commercial centre of Delhi, this is a series of graceful concentric colonnaded circles of shops and offices designed by Robert Tor Russell. At the centre, below a convex grassy exterior, is an underground air-conditioned market.
Head down the first section of Janpath.

5 Janpath

The most famous of the radial roads, Janpath is home to India's Central Cottage Industries Emporium (CCIE, two sites), and the roadside Tibetan

Market. The Government of India Tourist Office is on one side, and a little further on, the fine colonial Imperial Hotel has been given a new lease of life.
Turn on to Tolstoy Marg, continue to Barakhamba Rd, which leads back to India Gate via the Natural History Museum, and several cultural centres and auditoria on Copernicus Marg.

National Philatelic Museum Dak Bhavan, Sansad Marg. *Tel: (011) 2371 0154/2303 2451. Open: Mon–Fri 10am–5pm. Free.*
Natural History Museum FICCI Building, Barakhamba Rd. *Tel: (011) 2331 4849/2331 9173. Open: Tue–Sun 10am–5pm. Admission charge.*
No state building is open to the public, but the Mughal Gardens of the Rashtrapati Bhavan can be visited during Feb–Mar.

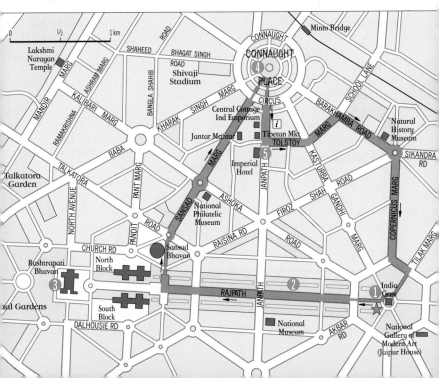

Walk: Old Delhi

Two of Old Delhi's most fascinating sights are linked by one of the largest, busiest, and most compelling markets in India; the atmosphere is at its best early in the evening when it is cooler, and the crowds are out in force. Although the route described keeps to the larger roads, take the opportunity to wander through the tiny side streets that make up the core of the market. The area is not large, so even if you get lost you should eventually emerge near a recognisable landmark.

Allow about one hour, plus browsing time.

The balconied Jain temple stands next to the white marble Sikh temple

Start beside the Lahore Gate of the Red Fort (see p38). Cross the open ground and the main road opposite. During Oct–Jan there is a fairground on this site and you may have to walk round it.

1 Chandni Chowk (Silver Street)

Also known as the Moonlit Bazaar, this was the main east–west thoroughfare of Shahjahanabad (founded 1638), a gracious boulevard with a canal and

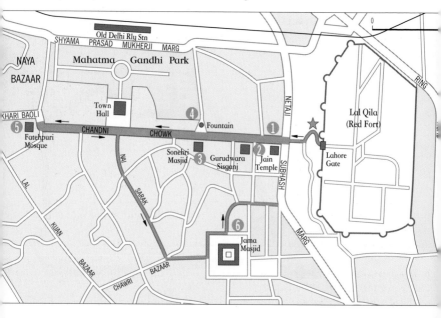

trees that became the commercial heart of India. Today, the street and its surrounding maze of alleys and passages are a heaving mass of humanity selling everything from plastic buckets and clothes, to exquisite gold jewellery and perfumed oils.

On the corner of Chandni Chowk and Netaji Subhash Marg (the main road) is a Jain temple.

2 Jain and Sikh temples

Belonging to the Digamber sect, the balconied Parshvanatha Jain temple was built in 1650, but has been restored, extended, and elaborated to such an extent that little of the original remains. It houses a bird hospital, and is lit up at night. Almost next door, on the left, the white marble Sikh Gurudwara Sisganj was built in honour of the guru, Teg Bahadur, beheaded by Emperor Aurangzeb in 1675. Nearby, the Kotwali (police station) witnessed the killing of the 1857 mutineers by the British.

The Sonehri Masjid is a little further along on the left.

3 Sonehri Masjid (Golden Mosque)

Built in 1722, this mosque was named for its copper-clad domes. In 1739, Delhi was invaded by the Persian king, Nadir Shah, who chose to use the roof as a vantage point from which to watch as his soldiers decimated Delhi, killing many thousands (reports range from 20,000 to 150,000), looting and torching most of the city.

4 The British influence

On the right-hand side of the road is a small enclave of the British Raj,

Chandni Chowk has been Main Street, Old Delhi, since 1638

consisting of an ornamental fountain, colonial-style Town Hall (1860–65), and the Mahatma Gandhi Park, which leads through to Old Delhi Railway Station.

Continue down Chandni Chowk to the far end, where a narrow arch leads through the line of the old city wall.

5 Fatehpuri Mosque

Marking the western end of Chandni Chowk, this large red sandstone mosque was built in 1650 by Begum Fatehpuri, one of Shah Jahan's wives. Just beyond it is the spice market (Khari Baoli).

Backtrack a little way up Chandni Chowk and turn right along Nai Sarak (the paper market). This road leads round the edge of the market alleys to the Jama Masjid.

6 Jama Masjid (Friday Mosque)

See p37.

The main entrance leads back to Netaji Subhash Marg. There are plenty of autos, cycles, rickshaws and taxis in the car park.

Tour: The many ages of Delhi

Most people talk of the seven cities of Delhi. However, there have definitely been up to 15 separate building periods, the area has been inhabited more or less continuously for about 3,500 years, and there is sketchy evidence of people around as far back as 15,000 BC. Most surviving monuments date from the 10th century AD onwards, and are found in the far south and in the northeast of the city. The following is a suggested chronological itinerary, but to visit these sites in order would not make geographical sense because of the huge distances in heavy traffic. (*See map, p53.*)
Allow two days to visit all the sites listed.

Detail from Qutb Minar, part of the legacy of Delhi's past

1 Indraprastha (15th century BC)
A legendary city of the great Hindu epic, the *Mahabharata*, the real-life prototype is thought to have been on roughly the same site as the **Purana Qila** (*see pp52–3*). No physical remains have been found, although the site has yielded pottery of the right age.

2 Lal Kot (late 10th century AD)
Although there are signs that it was inhabited as far back as the 8th century, the remaining walls of this once formidable citadel are considered to mark the first surviving city of Delhi, founded by the Rajput Tomar dynasty, and known at the time as **Dhilli** or **Dhillika** (the basis for the modern name). The city was captured and extended by the Chauhan family, under whom it became known as **Qila Rai Pithora**. In 1193, Qutbuddin Aibak

made it the centre of the first Muslim dynasty, and by the 13th century, the village of Mehrauli had sprung up here around the shrine of a Sufi saint, Qutb Sahib. The **Qutb Minar** complex (*see p44*) now stands on the spot.

3 Siri (1303)
The official second city of Delhi, Siri was laid out by Sultan Alauddin Khalji. Not much is known about it except that it was the first to be built from scratch by a Muslim ruler, and was fed by water from a vast tank known as the **Hauz Khas**, a little way from the city proper. Hauz Khas became a quaint complex of medieval buildings during Feroz Shah Tughlaq's reign (1351–88), and is much more interesting than Siri. He built a mosque and *madrasa* (religious training college), and his austere tomb is one of several inside.

Only the central court now marks the site of 14th-century Feroz Shah Kotla

4 Tughlaqabad (1321–25)

An octagonal sprawl of 6.5km of 10–15m-high rubble-filled walls and 13 gates, the dramatic fortress of Tughlaqabad was built by Ghiyasuddin Tughlaq (r.1321–25), and only inhabited during those five years. On a rocky outcrop on the edge of south Delhi, its massive ruins are now virtually deserted, except for a few goats and many monkeys, and prove an excellent site for picnics and walking (in groups). On the opposite side of the road is a small walled enclosure, joined to the fort by a causeway that crossed an artificial lake. Inside is the self-built domed **tomb of Ghiyasuddin**, his wife and son Mohammad-bin-Tughlaq, who had his father killed. He also built the small fort

of **Adilabad**, the ruins of which can be seen on a nearby hill.

5 Jahanpanah (early 14th century)

Once he had managed to get rid of his father (with an 'accidentally' collapsing canopy during a victory celebration), Mohammad-bin-Tughlaq (r.1325–51)

Hauz Khas access through Hauz Khas Village, off Aurobindo Marg.
Tughlaqabad 8km east of the Qutb Minar, Badarpur Rd.
Ferozabad (Feroz Shah Kotla) near the Raj Ghat, Bahadur Shah Zafar Marg.
Lodi Gardens Lodi Rd.
Purana Qila opposite the Crafts Museum, Pragati Maidan.
All the sites are open daily, sunrise–sunset. Admission charge for Purana Qila, Feroz Shah Kotla and the Red Fort.

went on to build yet another citadel, between Siri and Lal Kot, as a link between the two. Scattered walls remain of this structure, believed to be Delhi's fourth city.

6 Ferozabad (Feroz Shah Kotla (1354)

The Tughlaqs built a new capital for each new reign. Feroz Shah's contribution was the city of Ferozabad, of which only the central court remains, as much of the city was recycled to build Shahjahanabad. At the height of its glory, the city extended from Hauz Khas to the banks of the Yamuna. The surviving perimeter wall had four gates, one leading to the river. The structures inside include a vast *baoli* (stepped well), and a sort of stepped pyramid, built to display an Ashokan pillar moved to Delhi from Topra, 100km away, by Feroz Shah.

7 Lodi Gardens (late 15th–early 16th century)

This delightful park, laid out by Lady Willingdon in 1936, contains several small tombs and mosques belonging to the Sayyid and Lodi (1451–1526) dynasties, who first moved

their capital to Agra, and then lost their domain to the Mughals. Among the tombs, that of Mohammad Shah Sayyid (r.1434–44) and Sikander Lodi's (r.1489–1517) are similar, with an octagonal central chamber surrounded by arches and a high dome. The anonymous Shish Gumbad (Glass Dome) and Bara Gumbad (Big Dome) are square, and each has a false second storey. The mosque next door was built in 1494. The **Athpula**, a low multi-arched bridge over the lake, was probably built during Akbar's reign by a Muslim nobleman, Nawab Bahadur.

8 Purana Qila (1530–45)

This site has had several incarnations, beginning with **Indraprastha**. Remains from the Gupta, Rajput, and Delhi Sultanate periods have also been found. The Mughal emperor Humayun built his new city of **Dinpanah** (Asylum of Faith) here. In 1540 he was deposed by the Afghan, Sher Shah, who knocked it down and built the existing fort, **Shergarh**, with 2-km long walls and three main gates. Humayun completed the

ASHOKAN RELICS

The Mauryan emperor Ashoka (268–231 BC) was a relatively benevolent and very efficient father figure who created roads and rest houses, and sent Buddhist missionaries out to other areas of Asia. Across his kingdom, he scattered a series of pillars and rocks, carved in Brahmi script, both to record his achievements, and to exhort his subjects to behave well. The script was finally deciphered by James Princep in 1837.

Delhi's two Ashokan pillars now stand in the grounds of Feroz Shah Kotla, and beside the Hindu Rao Hospital, Rani Jhansi Marg. There is also a rock edict on an outcrop near Srinivaspuri, near the Ring Road past Lajpatnagar. Free admission.

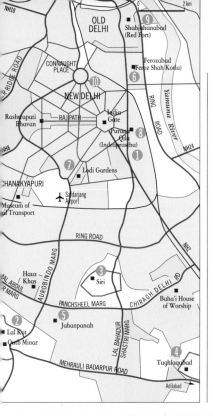

fort on regaining his throne in 1555, then fell down the steps of the **Sher Mandal**, the double-storey octagonal tower which he used as a library, to a tragic death. The richly ornamented **Qala-i-Kuhna Masjid** (Mosque of the Old Fort) was built by Sher Shah in 1541. There is a small site museum.

9 Shahjahanabad (1638–48)

This is the surviving city of Old Delhi, built by Shah Jahan of Taj Mahal fame. (*See p34 & pp48–9.*)

10 New Delhi (1931)

The British had made Calcutta (Kolkata) their capital in the 18th century. At the Delhi Durbar of 1911, King George V announced plans to move the capital back to Delhi. Sir Edwin Lutyens was hired to design it, and New Delhi was inaugurated in 1931 (*see pp46–7*).

Sir Edwin Lutyens' Rashtrapati Bhavan gates with the Ashoka lion emblem

Babur (r.1494–1530)
(1526 in India)

Babur (The Tiger), the conqueror of India, and the first Mughal emperor, was a great warrior, a diarist, an enthusiastic hunter and a lover of gardens who was little impressed by what he saw of his new territory. He died in the Rambagh Gardens, Agra, and is buried in Kabul, Afghanistan.

Humayun (r.1530–40 and 1555)

Humayun is remembered chiefly for his failures. In 1540, the Afghan leader Sher Shah usurped his empire, forcing the king to flee to Persia. He returned to power only a year before he fell down his library steps to his death in 1556. His main achievement was the introduction of Persian miniature painting whose influence, combined with native Indian skill, created the classic Mughal artistic tradition. He is buried in Delhi (see p36).

Akbar (r.1556–1605)

The greatest of the Mughals, Akbar came to the throne aged 13. He conquered massive new territories, including much of Rajasthan, created an efficient administrative system and an astute political hierarchy, introduced standard weights and measures, and expedient tax structures. Among his several wives was a Hindu Rajput princess from Jaipur, whom he married to prove his solidarity with the Rajputs. He was enormously liberal for his time, promoting religious tolerance, abolishing slavery, and discontinuing enforced *sati* (see p19). He created his own short-lived hybrid religion,

Din-i-Ilahi, which combined elements of Islam, Hinduism, Christianity and Zoroastrianism. His reign is also outstanding for its achievements in art, architecture, music and literature. He died in Agra and is buried in nearby Sikandra (see pp64–5).

Jahangir (r.1605–27)

Jahangir (Conqueror of the World) contributed little to the political or territorial expansion of the empire, and is best known for his self indulgences. He was also a connoisseur of the arts. His favourite wife, Nur Jahan (Light of the World), was a woman of staggering beauty and intellect who effectively ran the empire. He is buried in Pakistan.

Shah Jahan (r.1628–58)

Shah Jahan (Ruler of the World) inherited a near bankrupt empire. Nevertheless, he succeeded in expanding his territory southwards across the Deccan Peninsula, and became the greatest of the Mughal builders, creator of the Taj Mahal (see pp60–61), and patron of the arts.

Shah Jahan spent the last eight years of his life (1658–66) imprisoned by his son within his own fort in Agra, gazing down the river at the mausoleum where he was eventually to be buried alongside his favourite wife, Mumtaz Mahal.

Aurangzeb (r.1658–1707)

An imposing but ruthless character, Aurangzeb (Ornament of the Throne) fought his brothers for supremacy (later executing them), then overthrew his father. A series of military campaigns extended the empire into the deep south of India, but Aurangzeb was a puritanical extremist who treated the Hindus harshly, often destroying their temples and replacing them with mosques. His policies created hatred and led eventually to a series of insurrections that fragmented the Mughal Empire. He is buried in Aurangabad, near Mumbai.

Facing page: Akbar (top) was a liberal emperor, and Jahangir a connoisseur of the arts
Above: Humayun, like all the Mughal emperors, has a truly palatial tomb
Above right: Life at court was luxurious, surrounded by fine gardens, art and beautiful women

Agra

Standing on the banks of the Yamuna River, Agra is a city of over a million inhabitants. Like Delhi, it has been inhabited for thousands of years, and takes its place in history and the great Hindu legends. Sikander Lodi moved his imperial capital here in 1504, and for the next 150 years, under the rule of the early Mughal emperors, the fame of its sumptuous court spread across the world. In the 1650s, power moved back to Delhi. Today, in the large and chaotic city, a handful of superlative buildings remain as ghosts of its past glory.

The elaborate central pillar of Diwan-i-Khas, the Hall of Private Audience, in the Red Fort complex, Agra

Agra is 196km south of Delhi, with good road, rail, and air connections. Government of India Tourist Office: 191 The Mall. Tel: (0562) 2226 378;

Uttar Pradesh Government Tourist Office: 64 Taj Rd. Tel: (0562) 2360 517; Tourist Reception Centre: Agra Cantonment Station. Tel: (0562) 2368 596.

The tiny but perfect tomb of Itmad-ud-Daulah proved inspirational to builders of the Taj Mahal

Itmad-ud-Daulah's Tomb

Composed of pure white marble inlaid with precious stones and covered with filigree screens, this tomb seems as fragile as an ivory jewellery box. Built between 1622 and 1628 by Nur Jahan (wife of Jahangir) for her Persian father, Mirza Ghiasuddin Beg (Itmad-ud-Daulah), it stands in formal *charbagh* gardens and is as intensely, yet delicately, decorated inside as it is on the exterior. *Aligarh Rd (east bank). Open: sunrise–sunset. Admission charge.*

Ram Bagh Gardens

Laid out by Emperor Babur in 1528, this is the earliest surviving example of Mughal gardens in India. However, in spite of a host of attendant gardeners, the lack of water and willpower has led to its virtual demise, leaving only faint outlines of its former splendour among the overgrown bushes and broken pavilions.
Aligarh Rd (east bank). Locked, but officially open sunrise to sunset; wait for a gardener. Admission charge.

Agra

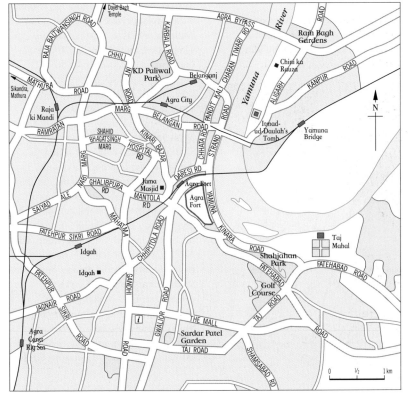

Red Fort

Although Babur's capital was Agra, and Humayun also built in this city, it was Akbar who created Agra's magnificent fort on the site of an existing citadel. Roughly crescent-shaped, the complex of courtly buildings is enclosed by a massive 20-m high curtain wall, faced by decorative red sandstone. An outer ring was added by Aurangzeb. It is very similar to the Delhi Red Fort, but although only one-third its size, gives an impression of being larger and more imposing.

Shah Jahan filled the Red Fort with graceful, fluted marble pavilions

Akbar's Palace

Immediately on the right as you enter through Amar Singh Gate are two interlinked red sandstone buildings, the

Site Plan

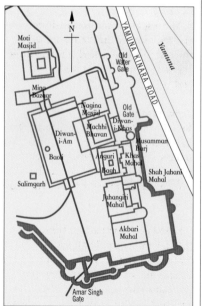

Akbari Mahal and the **Jahangiri Mahal** – the largest private residence in the complex, built for Akbar's son, Jahangir. These royal apartments (1570) are all that remain of Akbar's original buildings, and show his preferred eclectic style of design, with Hindu, Mughal and Persian details.

Shah Jahan's Palaces

Shah Jahan demolished or redesigned the rest of the buildings, giving the complex a palatial rather than a military character. He used a softer and more flowing style, with creamy marble and inlay, stucco, paint and gilt, instead of the hard-edged, sombre sandstone. The difference in atmosphere is startling as you walk through the prettily decorated **Shah Jahani Mahal** and enter the enchanting **Khas Mahal** (Private Palace), its decor and gleaming copper roofs carefully restored. This was a private play area for the emperor and his women, overlooking the **Anguri Bagh** (Grape Garden), a formal jigsaw-patterned Mughal garden filled with fountains and water channels, and surrounding screens ensuring privacy.

Beyond this is the **Musamman Burj**, a delicate octagonal tower which is not only one of the most beautiful buildings in the Fort, but the most tragic. Shah Jahan spent much of his eight-year imprisonment here, and died on the balcony, gazing down the river to the Taj Mahal. The view is superb, when not marred by the dust and pollution haze. The marble courtyard is marked out with a *pachisi* (Indian backgammon) board, played, it is said, using dancing girls as pieces.

Further ahead, at first-floor level, are the **Diwan-i-Khas** (Hall of Private Audience), built in 1635–7, the emperor's private chapel, the **Mina Masjid** (Heavenly Mosque) and the **harem** (women's quarters).

At ground level, the silver-spangled **Sheesh Mahal** (Hall of Mirrors) is now badly damaged, but was once magnificent, filled with the sound of running water, while oil lamps reflected a thousand times in its glittering tiny mirrors. It led into the **Machhi Bhavan** (Fish Building), which gained its name from the central tank stocked with fish for angling. The surrounding rooms later became offices, while the courtyard was used to receive visiting dignitaries. Beside this were the emperor's baths and the **Nagina Masjid** (Gem Mosque), made of pure white marble, and used by the ladies of the harem. On the far side, facing out into the public areas of the fort, lay the **Diwan-i-Am** (Hall of Public Audience), its vast courtyard now incongruously occupied by the tomb of John Colvin, former Lieutenant-

Agra fort pavilion looking out across the Yamuna on to the Taj Mahal

Governor of the Northwest Provinces. (d.1858).

The rest of the fort is closed, and you can only see the domes of the supposedly perfect, marble **Moti Masjid** (Pearl Mosque), built between 1646 and 1653.

Jama Masjid

Built in 1648 by Shah Jahan's favourite daughter, Jahanara Begum, this beautiful sandstone and marble mosque was intended to link the palace and the town. It stands near the Delhi Gate (now closed; no access from the fort).

The Red Fort is on the west bank, about 2.5km north of the Taj Mahal, off Yamuna Kinara Rd. Open: daily sunrise–sunset. Admission charge (Fri free). Jama Masjid, on Jama Masjid Rd, behind Agra Fort Station. Free admission.

Taj Mahal

O Soul, thou art at rest.
Return to the Lord, at peace with Him and He at
peace with you.

89th chapter of the Quran,
engraved above the Great Gate of the Taj Mahal

SAFE FROM HARM

After the decline of the Mughal empire, the Taj, too, suffered neglect. Lord Bentinck, Governor General (1828–35) planned to dismantle and auction it bit by bit, but could not find enough buyers. It was Lord Curzon, Viceroy, 1899–1905, who restored it to its former glory. In recent years, the building has begun to suffer appallingly from the corrosive effects of air pollution. However, government's restoration efforts and relocation of Agra's industry far from the city will hopefully protect India's most cherished monument from harm.

For all the pictures and all the words written about it, the sight of that first glow as the minarets of the Taj Mahal capture the pearly pink of early dawn is still breathtaking. Even when swarming with tourists, the monument remains one of the most beautiful and romantic buildings in the whole world.

Just as the captivating first impression of the Taj seen from the gateway becomes one of imposing grandeur, the atmosphere alters with the changing light, so try and return several times, particularly at dawn and sunset. Also head across to the far bank to see its magical reflection in the Yamuna River.

Monument to love

Mumtaz Mahal (Chosen One of the Palace) was a title given to Arjumand Banu, the favourite wife of Emperor Shah Jahan (*see p55*). She died in 1631,

aged 39, during the birth of her 14th child. They had been married for 17 years. Her grieving husband set about creating for her the perfect mausoleum. It took 20,000 workmen, among them the Persian architect, Isa Khan, and nearly 22 years to complete the task.

The tomb is set in a classical *charbagh* (*see p36*), and surrounded by a high sandstone wall with three gates. There is a small museum in the west gate house. On either side of the central monument are identical red sandstone pavilions; that on the left (west) is a mosque, the one on the right is a copy, built for the sake of symmetry.

The Taj Mahal is a perfect example of the concise geometry and symmetry of Islamic architecture. It stands on a high marble plinth with four minarets, one at each corner, enhancing the sense of containment and perfect balance. All the elements of Islamic design are here: arches, minarets, the onion dome and calligraphy in black inlay work around the entrances. The mausoleum itself is constructed from white marble brought from Jodhpur (300km away). The entire building was inlaid with delicate *pietra dura* floral patterns, using precious and semi-precious stones including jade, lapis lazuli, diamonds and mother of pearl –

from places as far away as Baghdad, China and Russia. Shah Jahan is buried beside his wife in an underground chamber (closed to visitors). An exquisite tomb chamber covers the crypt below.

Taj Rd. Open: daily sunrise–sunset. Admission & photo charge. Take a torch to see clearly inside. Night viewings: five nights a month; tickets must be bought 24 hours in advance at the entrance.

The Taj Mahal is a unique example of perfect symmetry unlike any other building in the world

Agra environs

FATEHPUR SIKRI

In 1568 the much married but childless Emperor Akbar (*see p54*) asked a Sufi mystic, Sheik Salim Chishti, living in Sikri village, for help. Shortly afterwards, his first son Salim (Jahangir) was born. In gratitude, between 1570 and 1582, Akbar built his administrative capital around Chishti's abode. For 14 years it was one of the most splendid cities in the world, but water was short, the emperor's wars kept him away, and the city was abandoned. It is a compelling place, perfectly preserved even after 400 years. There are two sections: the

mosque complex and the palace, an intricate series of pavilions and courtyards.

Jama Masjid

An 84-room colonnade encloses the mosque and its vast courtyard. Persian and Hindu design elements are evident in the structures. Entry from the village is through the massive **Buland Darwaza** (Victory Gate), built to commemorate Akbar's victory in Gujarat. Beside it, a deep well invites local children to display their diving talents. The **Badshahi Darwaza** (King's Gate) to

Fatehpur Sikri

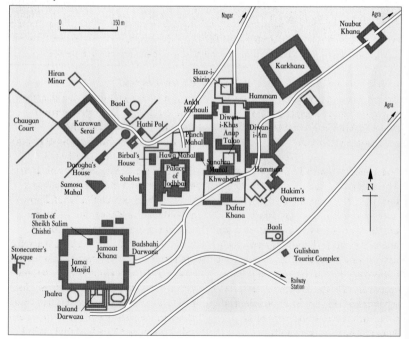

Sunahra Mahal seen from the balcony of the Panch Mahal – a blend of Hindu and Islamic styles

its east, was the king's entrance. Behind the mosque, a gateway overlooks a spiky tower, the **Hiran Minar**, tomb of Akbar's favourite elephants (who were made to crush wrongdoers).

Sheikh Salim Chishti's Dargah

The tomb of Akbar's benefactor, who died in 1571, was completed in 1580 in red sandstone. In 1606, Jahangir's brother clad the building in marble, and added the superb latticed screens, each carved from a single block. People of all faiths come here to tie red and yellow cotton threads to the screens and pray for parenthood. Tombs of members of the saint's family lie in front of his **Jamaat Khana** (prayer hall).

Palace complex

As you enter past the ticket office, the area to the left is the **Haram Sara** (harem). Straight ahead, the freestanding **Sunahra Mahal** (Maryam's House) was the home of Akbar's Christian wife, Maryam Makani. To the left, the rather forbidding rectangular building, with a blue tiled roof, known as **Jodhabai's Palace** (after Akbar's Hindu wife), provided the women's main accommodation. Behind it are the old **stables** and the king's Hindu prime minister **Birbal's House** (some say, the home of Akbar's two senior wives). Back inside, a series of small courtyards leads through the harem gardens to the open-sided five-tiered **Panch Mahal** (Wind

is dominated inside by an ornate pillar surrounded by flying arches. The emperor sat in the centre, with a clear view of his ministers seated along the bridges. On the far right is the **Diwan-i-Aam** (Hall of Public Audience).

To the right, steps lead into the **Anup Talao** (Peerless Pool) courtyard, where Akbar would sit surrounded by perfumed water, while Tansen, his brilliant court musician, would sing. Behind that was the **Khwabgah** (House of Dreams) and his private apartments. *37km west of Agra, on the Jaipur road. Open: sunrise–sunset. Admission charge. Start early. (Jama Masjid is free.)*

MATHURA

As the birthplace of Lord Krishna, Mathura is an immensely important Hindu pilgrimage centre. Several surrounding villages, including **Brindaban**, **Gokul**, **Mahaban** and **Goverdhan**, are also associated with important events in the god's life, and the area is littered with thousands of small temples, few of any architectural significance. The **Archaeological Museum** has a superb collection of sculpture, terracotta, bronze and coins (5th century BC to 12th century AD). *58km north of Agra, on the Yamuna River and main Delhi Rd. Reached by road and rail. Archaeological Museum: Dampier Nagar. Open: Tue–Sun 10.30am–4.30pm; Apr–Jun 7.30am–12.30pm. Free admission.*

Hindu pilgrims visiting a temple in Mathura, birthplace of Lord Krishna

Tower), a pavilion from which the ladies could watch the court. There's an excellent view from the top across the huge **Pachisi Court**, marked with a type of backgammon board, played, according to legend, using servant girls as pieces. To the left are the **Ankh Michauli** (Treasury), and the **Diwan-i-Khas** (Hall of Private Audience), which

SIKANDRA
(Akbar's Mausoleum)

Emperor Akbar (*see p54*) began building his own magnificent mausoleum in 1602 in this suburb of Agra. It was completed by Jahangir in 1613. Composed of local red sandstone and marble, the walled complex has four gates, three of them dummies. The imposing entrance gate is topped by white marble cupolas and minarets which echo those of the Taj. It leads into the *charbagh* gardens, now inhabited by over-friendly monkeys.

On a raised platform at the centre stands the superb five-storey, stepped monument (its upper levels now closed to visitors). A small strip of the once

fabulously painted, central, domed echo chamber has now been restored for effect. The low entrance door to the actual grave means that visitors are forced to bow their heads as they enter, in respect. Outside, the buildings are all richly decorated with grey, black, white and yellow Rajasthani marble inlay. Recurring decorative themes include the round Hindu cupola, the minarets of Islam, and the Christian cross.

Mathura Rd, 8km northwest of Agra. Open: daily sunrise–sunset. Admission charge.

The graceful dignity of Akbar's mausoleum at Sikandra is exemplified by the magnificent entrance gate

Rajasthan

'*The poorest Rajput of this day
retains all the pride of ancestry, often
his sole inheritance; he scorns to hold
the plough or to use his lance but on
horseback. In these aristocratic ideas
he is supported by his reception
amongst his superiors, and the respect
paid to him by his inferiors. The
honours and privileges, and the
gradations of rank, amongst the
vassals of the Rana's house, exhibit a
highly artificial and refined state of
society. Each of the superior rank is
entitled to a banner, kettle-drums
preceded by heralds and silver maces,
with peculiar gifts and personal
honours, in commemoration of some
exploit of their ancestors.*'

JAMES TODD

Annals and Antiquities of Rajasthan, 1829

The international boundaries on this map are neither purported
to be correct nor authenticated by Survey of India directives.

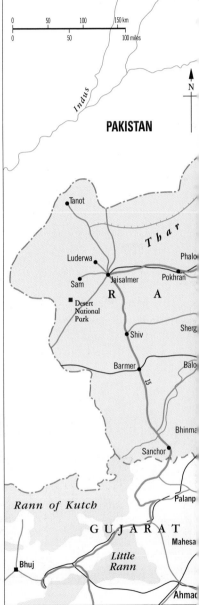

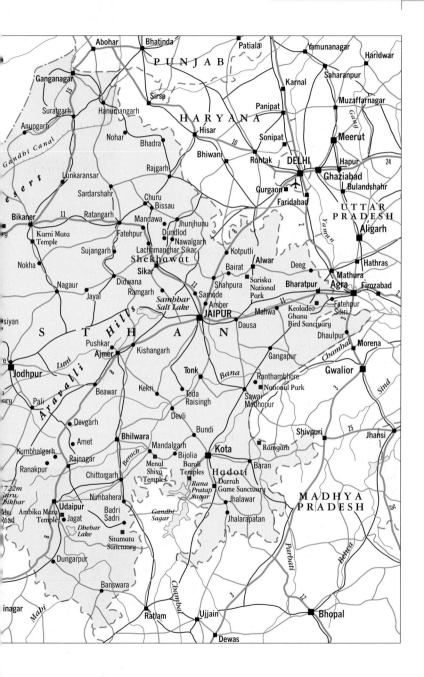

Ajmer

Ajmer was founded by Raja Ajai Pal Chauhan in the 7th century. In 1193, Prithviraj, last of the Chauhan rulers, lost the town to Mohammed Ghori, and it became part of the Delhi Sultanate. After centuries of passing between the Muslims and Rajputs, the town was captured by Akbar in 1556 who made it his own Rajput base. Jahangir and Shah Jahan both lived here for some time. As a result, modern Ajmer is a real anomaly – a primarily Muslim holy city at the heart of die-hard Hindu Rajasthan. With the collapse of the great Mughals, it became a territory ruled directly by the British in 1818, whose greatest legacy to Ajmer was Mayo College, a school for Rajput princes.

Flower sellers do brisk business around the *dargah*

Ajmer is 135km west of Jaipur and 205km east of Jodhpur. Tourist Information Office: Hotel Khadim, Savitri Girls College Rd. Tel: (0145) 52426.

Adhai-Din-ka-Jhonpra

Qutbuddin Aibak, Mohammed Ghori's commander (*see p9*), built this dramatic mosque in 1200, supposedly in two and a half days (*adhai-din*). He demolished a Jain Sanskrit college built 50 years before and reused the pieces. Each of the tall ornate columns is made up of three Hindu pillars. The superb façade, with seven massive arches, each different from the other and floridly inscribed with Quranic script, was added by Iltutmish in about 1213.

250m north of the Dargah Sharif, Nalla Bazaar. Free admission during daytime.

Akbar's Palace/Museum

Also known as the Daulat Khana (Abode of Wealth), this red sandstone palace was built by Akbar as his local base in Rajputana. It was used as an arsenal by the British from 1818 to 1862, and now houses a very ordinary government museum, with miniature paintings, Mughal arms and 4th- to 12th-century temple statuary.

Prithviraj Marg. Open: 10am–4.30pm. Closed: Fri. Admission charge.

The magnificent Dargah Sharif in Ajmer

Buland Darwaza, the entrance gate to Dargah Sharif

Ana Sagar

Nearly 13km in circumference, this beautiful artificial lake was built between 1135 and 1150 by Anaji Chauhan. Centuries later, the Mughal emperors Jahangir and Shah Jahan laid out a lush pleasure garden, and built a series of delightful (recently restored) marble pavilions along the bank. Do read the extraordinarily long list of prohibitions on the park signs.
Circular Rd. Open: daily 7am–10pm. Free admission.

Dargah Sharif

The *dargah* of Muslim Sufi saint, Khwaja Moinuddin Chishti (1142–1236), has become a global focus of Islamic pilgrimage. Born in Persia, the saint came to India with Mohammed Ghori, settled in Ajmer, and founded the Chishtiya monastic order dedicated to protecting the poor. The complex surrounding his magnificent domed marble tomb, with silver rails and gates, was founded by the Delhi Sultan, Iltutmish, and completed by Humayun. Shah Jahan built the inner marble mosque, and Akbar the mosque in the outer court. Two vast cauldrons are used to feed pilgrims during the annual Urs Ajmer Sharif festival.
Dargah Bazaar. Free admission.

Mayo College

One of the leading residential public schools in India today, Mayo College was established in 1875 by Lord Mayo, to provide an Anglicised education to Rajput princes. The school is housed in an outstanding example of Indo-Saracenic architecture.

The holy town of Pushkar has the only temple to Brahma in India

Circular Rd. Tel: (0145) 660697. Visit with permission from the Principal.

Nasiyan (Soni) Jain temple

Behind the temple proper, built in 1864 (closed to non-Jains), the two-storey Svarna Nagari Hall houses a fantastic gilded model depicting the Jain concept of the universe (*see pp22–3*). It took 25 years to complete, and was first displayed in 1895.

At the centre of the flat earth in the model stands Mount Sumeru, surrounded by the 13 continents and 13 oceans described in Jain scriptures. Above fly the *vimanas* (airships) of the gods, coming to celebrate the five great events (*kalyanakas*) – conception, birth, renunciation, attainment of omniscience and salvation – in the life of Lord Rishabdev, first of the 24 *tirthankaras*.
Anok Chowk, Prithviraj Marg. Open: daily, summer 8am–5.30pm; winter 8am–5pm. Admission charge. Buy the small guidebook for a detailed explanation of the model.

Taragarh (Star Fort)

A ruinous rectangular fort on top of a 250-m high hill, the 7th-century Taragarh is said to be the earliest Rajput hill fort in existence, although most of its surviving components were added considerably later. It was used as a sanatorium during British rule.

Buildings of interest include a mosque and the shrine of Miran Sayyid Hussain, a Muslim saint. There are wonderful views from the top.

3km west of the city, from Nalla Bazaar. Allow one and a half hours for the steep climb if you want to walk.

AJMER ENVIRONS
Pushkar

For most of the year, Pushkar is a tiny peaceful town set in the foothills round a deep blue lake, which is said to have been formed by a falling petal when Brahma slew the demon Vijra Nabh with a lotus. Brahma went on to perform *yagna* (sacrifice) here, marrying a local girl. His wife, Savitri, was furious, and cursed him, saying that from now on, he would not be worshipped anywhere else but here in Pushkar. Thus, in this little town is the only temple to Brahma in the whole of India, sitting among 400 other temples, numerous ashrams and pavilions, and 52 *ghats* crowded around the lake.

Pushkar has a steady trickle of pilgrims, and it is popular with budget travellers who come here to laze and recuperate. All that changes every October/November, however, when for two weeks, the little town seethes with hundreds of thousands of people, cattle, camels and horses, gathered together for the **Pushkar Mela**, Rajasthan's biggest and most colourful fair (*see p25*).

12km north of Ajmer. No tourist office, except during the fair. The town is alcohol-free and strictly vegetarian.

The peaceful town of Pushkar

Alwar

Alwar, on Rajasthan's borders, has a noble pedigree, being mentioned as a powerful kingdom in the *Mahabharata* (c.1500 BC), and also by the Chinese traveller, Hiuen Tsang (7th century AD). For centuries the area belonged to Jaipur, and then Bharatpur, but in 1771, Pratap Singh, a minor relative of the Kachhwaha family, broke away and set up his own kingdom, which rapidly became known for its spectacular ostentation, culminating in such glories as a gold car and solid silver dining table.

The cenotaph of Musi Maharani ki Chhatri

202km south of Delhi, and 141km north of Jaipur, reached by road and rail. Tourist Reception Centre: Opp. railway station. Tel: (0144) 21868.

Bala Qila Fort

Sitting 300m above the town, this superbly sited ancient fort offers fabulous views. It has massive 13-km long walls, with 66 defensive towers and seven gates, and a frescoed palace complex added in the late 18th century. Unfortunately, it now houses a police transmitter, and access requires special permission.

Access on foot up a steep path, or by car. Ask for written permission from the Superintendent of Police, City Palace.

Vinay Vilas (City Palace)

Built by the victorious Pratap Singh in 1793, the architecture of this vast and magnificent palace, set around two huge courtyards, shows a strong Mughal influence. Most of the buildings are now used as the city's administrative offices. On the first floor, the **Government Museum** has some rare exhibits, although it is badly maintained. It contains exhibits ranging from royal footwear and a stuffed tiger, to an impressive and valuable collection of 18th- and 19th-century miniature paintings – including erotica of the home-grown Alwar school. Among a great many rare manuscripts are a copy of the *Mahabharata*, written on a 75-m long scroll, the *Babur Namah* (the emperor Babur's autobiography), and works in Sanskrit, Arabic, Persian, and Urdu (the court language, derived from Hindi and Persian). The armoury includes some magnificent jewelled weapons, among them the swords of Akbar and Jahangir, and the armour of Mohammed Ghori.

Cenotaph and tank

Surrounded by numerous steps and pavilions, this large, startlingly pea-green tank provided the City Palace's main water supply, used for drinking, bathing, and laundry. To one side stands **Musi Maharani ki Chhatri**, an elegant

cenotaph built by Vinay Singh in 1815 to the mistress of Bakhtawar Singh who committed *sati* (*see p19*) here.
Near Collectorate. Free access to the courtyard, tank and cenotaph. Museum open: 10am–5pm. Closed: Fri. Admission charge.

ALWAR ENVIRONS
Bairat

Bairat has one of the oldest archae-ological sites in Rajasthan, lying atop a spectacular boulder-strewn hilltop with shrines to Bhima and Hanuman (heroes of the *Mahabharata* and *Ramayana*), the remains of a Buddhist *chaitya* hall (monastery), and a rock edict of the emperor Ashoka (3rd century BC).
66km west of Alwar on the road to Jaipur. Free access.

Sariska

This is one of Rajasthan's largest, most important and beautiful national parks.
For details, see p143.

Siliserh Lake

This truly delightful horseshoe lake covers an area of 10.5sq km in a bowl of rocky hills. Beside it is a tiny water palace said to have been built by Maharaja Vinay Singh in 1810 for his young, homesick wife, a beautiful village girl who insisted on living in sight of her family. It is now an isolated and peaceful tourist bungalow – good for watching birds, and for a rest en route to Alwar and Sariska.
13km southwest of Alwar, off the Sariska road. Free admission. Boat trips and pedaloes for hire, sunrise to sunset.

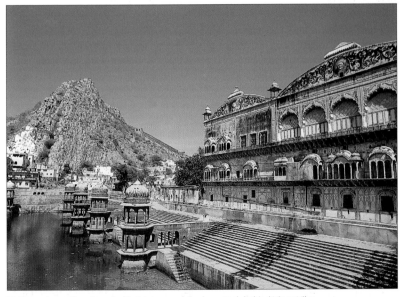

Platforms topped by elegant *chhatris* surround the huge tank behind Vinay Vilas

Bharatpur

Once capital of the tiny kingdom of Mewat, Bharatpur's glory years began – and ended – with the 18th-century Jat ruler, Maharaja Suraj Mal. Defying even the powerful Mughals, he sacked the Delhi and Agra forts, coming away with trophies such as the massive gates of Agra Fort which he installed at his summer palace at nearby Deeg. Bharatpur's superlative bird sanctuary is now its main attraction; few stray into the fort, built by Suraj Mal, or the busy little atmospheric market town.

Animals can also be seen at the Keoladeo Ghana Bird Sanctuary

182km south of Delhi, 54km west of Agra, and 174km east of Jaipur, reached from all three by road and rail. Tourist Information Office: Saras Circle Tourist Bungalow, on the Agra road.
Tel: (05644) 222542.

Keoladeo Ghana Bird Sanctuary

In 1733 the Bharatpur maharaja dammed a nearby irrigation canal to create a marshland breeding ground for birds. A stone tablet in the reserve details the staggering number of ducks blasted from the sky (up to 4,273 in one day during a 1938 shoot for Viceroy Linlithgow). The 29sq km area, about half of it marshland, became a national park in 1983. Now home to over 375 different species, Bharatpur is one of the finest bird sanctuaries in the world, and has a thriving animal population as well. It is utterly compelling even for those with no real interest in feathered creatures.
6km from Bharatpur. Tel: (05644) 222777. Open: sunrise–sunset. Admission & photo charge. See also pp76–7 & pp142–3.

Lohagarh (Iron Fort)

In 1732 work began on this vast and seemingly impregnable fort, with an outer packed mud and rubble wall 11km long. In 1805 the British failed to penetrate the defences after a four-month siege, but the maharaja nevertheless became the first Rajput prince to sign a treaty with them. Lying within the old inner wall are three palaces, only the oldest of which is open to the public. Built on three sides of a rectangle, and surrounding a sunken *hammam*, this palace now houses a rather sad **government museum** which contains some interesting arms, and 1st- and 2nd-century sculptures. Most of the fort walls have been destroyed.
Within the fort, access from town centre, via Mathura Gate. Open: Sat–Thur 10am–4.30pm. Admission charge.

BHARATPUR ENVIRONS
Deeg

The massive **citadel** was built in 1730 by the Jat ruler, Sural Mal, and dismantled by the British in 1804. Only the 28-m high wall remains. In 1768 the maharaja built himself a romantic summer **water palace** of rich yellow stone next door. The central building, the **Gopal Bhawan**, is flanked on either side by barge-shaped pavilions. In front are lush gardens, and behind it is a huge, pea-green tank, the **Gopal Sagar**, still used as a water supply by locals.

The palace has survived virtually intact, furnished with its moth-eaten tigers and billiard table, photos and various Mughal souvenirs, such as beds and a marble swing, looted from the Red Forts in Agra and Delhi.

The most fascinating aspect of all, considering the palace's close proximity to the desert, is the maharaja's obsession with water. The gardens are filled with nearly 2,000 fountains, with tricks and hidden devices, as well as huge set pieces, all designed to create an artificial monsoon. The **Keshav Bhavan** pavilion used jets of water to roll stone balls on the roof and recreate the sound of thunder. For the maharaja's birthday celebrations, the fountains' pipes would be packed with dye, and the fountains flowed in rainbow hues. It takes so long to collect enough water for the extravaganza that the fountains now only play for three days a year, in the first week of August. Deeg is a refreshing stop en route to Bharatpur by car.

32km north of Bharatpur. There are no taxis in Bharatpur. Provide your own transport, or ask to borrow (hire) a private car.

Water palace open: daily 8am–noon, 1–7pm. Admission charge.

Pure fantasy, the palace of Deeg created an artificial monsoon for a thirsty desert prince

Peacocks and Parakeets

A gang of brilliant green parakeets screams across the city park, a scops owl tucks its head down for a day asleep and a collared dove coos softly to the dawn. The fields are dotted with ultra-white cattle egrets, scavenging for worms disturbed by the buffaloes' hooves. Bald-headed vultures huddle greedily around the village refuse dump, partridges and quails lurk plumply in the dusty undergrowth and myna birds squabble in a nearby tree. A little black-and-white-pied robin tilts its head as it watches the watchers, busy bee-eaters follow the honey trail, a little brown bulbul trills tunefully in the bushes and a gaggle of babblers chatters about nothing. A peacock, India's national bird, struts past an overgrown tomb, shrieking for his hens. High above, a dozen different raptors soar on the morning thermals, eagle-eyed above the scrub. The lakes and marshes provide a whole

Facing page above: treepies draw attention to themselves with their raucous call; below: the wild peacock is India's national bird; above: the tuneful bulbul; below: the licence badge of a park rickshaw-puller

new range of birds, ducks and geese, moorhens and jacanas, cormorants and darters, herons, storks and cranes. A speckled pond heron floats in perfect camouflage on a muddy pool, while just above, a kingfisher flashes turquoise through the dappled shade. A mated pair of grey and scarlet Sarus cranes, the world's largest birds of flight, stick close together as they feed, and, most dramatic of all, a twisted acacia tree bulges top-heavy with scores of nesting painted storks.

India as a whole is home to some 1,200 species of bird, of which at least 400 are found in and around Rajasthan. About 375 species are found in Bharatpur alone. It is a paradise for 'twitchers', the astounding range, drama and sheer numbers of its birds sufficient to convert even Alfred Hitchcock devotees.

Bikaner

After the foundation of Jodhpur (*see p112*), Jodha Rathore's second son, Bika, fought with his father and left court, heading north, deep into the desert. In 1488, he conquered Jangal Desh (wilderness) and founded his own kingdom of Bikaner. A hermit promised that his dynasty would rule safely for four and a half centuries, which took it neatly up to 1947. At Independence, Bikaner became the first Rajput kingdom to join the Indian union. Today, it is a thriving city with a population of about 450,000.

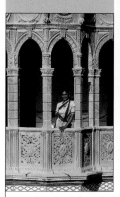

Lacy *jali* screens and ornamented stonework flourish in Junagarh Fort

243km north of Jodhpur and 321km northwest of Jaipur, reached by road and rail. Tourist Information Office: RTDC Hotel Dhola Maru, Poonam Singh Circle. Tel: (0151) 529621.

Ganga Golden Jubilee Museum

Founded in 1937 to mark the Golden Jubilee of Maharaja Ganga Singh, the museum moved into its current home in 1954. It has a fine collection, with pre-Harappan and Gupta period archaeological finds, paintings and photographs of the royal family, and local crafts including woodwork, glass, metal pots, *usta* (gilded leaf paintings) on camel hide, fine carpets woven by prisoners in Bikaner Jail, miniature paintings and a superb Jain marble statue of the goddess Saraswati. *Gandhi Park, Jaipur Rd. Open: 10am–4.30pm. Closed: Sun. Admission charge.*

Junagarh Fort

Built on flat ground in 1588 by Raja Rai Singh, one of Akbar's military allies, the rectangular fort has a 986-m long wall,
37 bastions and a 9-m wide moat. Successive rulers added to it over the next 300 years. Beside the yellow sandstone **Suraj Pol** (Sun Gate) stand lifesize statues of two warriors on elephants, whose heroic feats persuaded Akbar not to attack Bikaner. This is the only fort in Rajasthan that has never been conquered. It has now been carefully restored, and is filled with fabulous furniture and artistic treasures. The low thrones in the first courtyard were used during Holi when the public were allowed to bombard the maharaja with coloured water.

The second court is much larger, decorated with elephants and Chinese and Italian tiles. On the left, inside the pretty painted gilt- and glass-fronted pavilion (the **Karan Mahal**), is the silver throne of Karan Singh (1631–85), who built it to mark his victory over Aurangzeb. The **Anup Mahal** (Dancing Court) beyond, built by Anup Singh (1669–96) with 52 windows, one for each of his wives, was the public audience and coronation hall. Many of the surrounding rooms have exquisitely rich, gilded floral decorations. The *usta* style, which has become the town's signature, was introduced by Ali Raza and his family, Muslim artists from Jaisalmer, under the patronage of Karan Singh.

The **Phool Mahal** (Flower Palace), the **Chandra Mahal** (Moon Palace) – painted to look like marble *pietra dura* and filled with statues of the gods – and the **Sheesh Mahal** (Mirror Palace) were built by Rai Singh in the 16th century. In the private chamber in Chandra Mahal is the royal bed – too low for assassins to hide beneath, and so short,

the maharajas would always have their feet on the ground, ready to stand and fight. Many upper rooms have superb marble screens which allowed the *purdahed* (veiled) women to watch the entertainment without being seen. Ganga Singh's 19th-century palace houses an excellent museum and armoury, including elephant howdahs, palanquins and a biplane from World War II which he received as a signatory to the Versailles Treaty. There are fine views from the roof.

Fort Rd. Open: daily 10am–4.30pm. Admission & photo charge. Guided tours only.

View across Bikaner from the maharaja's private apartments

Karni Mata Temple, home to sacred rats

Lalgarh Palace

Designed by Sir Swinton Jacob, and built by Maharaja Ganga Singh in 1902, this red sandstone palace is still occupied by the royal family, but most of it is now a hotel. The **Sadul Museum's** collection of royal memorabilia includes 34,000 photographs of life at court. The **Anup Sanskrit Library** houses valuable manuscripts, many saved by Anup Singh from Golconda and Bijapur in 1687. It is open on request.
3km north on Lalgarh Palace Rd. Tel: (0151) 540201. Museum open: Thur–Tue 10am–4pm. Admission charge.

Old Town

Centred on Rao Bikaji's original fort, the surviving 18th-century walls of the old town were built on the 15th-century fortifications. Within the fort are two early 16th-century Hindu temples dedicated to Lakshmi Nath and Ganesh, (closed to non-Hindus), the sculpted **Chintamani Jain Temple** and the magnificently painted **Bhandasar Jain Temple** (1571), dedicated to Sumatinath. From the roof there is a view of the domes, the old town, and the **Bikaji-ki-Tekri**, cremation ground of the early rulers.
6km southwest of Junagarh Fort, along MG Rd. Bhandasar and Chintamani Jain temples open: daily 7–11am & 5–7pm. Free admission but photo charge.

BIKANER ENVIRONS
Camel Research Farm

Bikaner is famous for its camels (*see p146*). In 1975 the central government set up this station to research their habits, and create a superior breeding stock. The large herds include many calves.
9km southeast of Bikaner. Open: 3–5pm. Closed: Sun. Admission charge.

KARNI MATA

Durga, the goddess of war, came down to earth as Karni Mata for 151 years, six months and two days. Renowned as a miracle worker, she married a member of the ruling Charan family. One version of the legend says her husband's family laughed at her powers, refusing to believe in her divine nature. Goaded beyond reason, she turned them into rats. The other version is that they came to her when the young son of one of the brothers died. Karni Mata pleaded with Yama, God of Death, and the child was brought back to life. In exchange, however, all members of the Charan family have to live one life as a rat between their human incarnations. The thousands of rather mangy rats in the Deshnok (Karni Mata) temple are, therefore, treated with great deference as honorary humans, fed by hand on sugar and grain by the many pilgrims.

Devi Kund Sagar and cenotaphs

The earliest memorial in this royal cremation ground is to Kalyan Mal, who died in 1573; the latest is that of Karni Singh (an Olympics rifle-shooting contestant), who died in 1988. Other *chhatris* (canopies) of note include those of Anup Singh (d.1696), the *sati*, Maharani Deep Kanwar (d.1825), worshipped as a goddess and reformer Ganga Singh (d.1943).
8km south of city, near Camel Research Farm. Free admission.

Gajner Sanctuary

Once a royal hunting preserve, the area around the lake and 18th-century palace (built by Maharaja Gaj Singh) is now an animal and bird sanctuary, and winter breeding ground for the Siberian imperial sand grouse. There are also black buck, cheetal, sambar and *nilgai.*
35km west of Bikaner, on the Jaisalmer road. Tel: (0151) 55063 (Gajner Palace Hotel). Admission charge.

Karni Mata temple

This 17th-century temple, with its vast silver doors and gold umbrella, is a popular place of pilgrimage, but is not for the squeamish. Within the walls live thousands of sacred rats who play over your toes. The fine for killing one is the donation of a gold replica of it to the temple.
Deshnok, 32km southwest of Bikaner on the Jodhpur road. Free admission, except noon–4pm (camera charge).

The elaborately decorated interior of Bhandasar Jain Temple

Chittorgarh

Hilltop Chittorgarh is one of the earliest and most dramatic of Rajasthan's great citadels, capital of Mewar from AD 728 to 1567, and a symbol of Rajput heroism. The fort was sacked three times, and each time the men marched out to be massacred in a final hopeless battle, leaving their women to perform *jauhar* (mass self immolation), rather than succumb to the enemy. Finally, in 1567, Akbar triumphed, leaving 8,000 dead. He razed the fort, and it has been in ruins ever since.

PADMINI

Word of Queen Padmini's beauty reached Sultan Alauddin Khalji of Delhi, who became obsessed with seeing her, and besieged Chittor. Eventually, to end the conflict, he was allowed to see her reflection in a silver mirror. Enflamed by the brief glimpse, he ambushed her husband and held him to ransom. Padmini capitulated, and a procession of 700 veiled 'women' wound its way down to the Sultan's camp. Once inside, the Rajput soldiers threw off their disguise, routed the Muslim troops and rescued their king. The furious Sultan attacked again with greater success. This time, the women of the court committed *jauhar*, leaving Alauddin as the conqueror of ashes.

Walls and gates

The fort occupies an area of about 280 hectares (700 acres) along the crest of a 152-m high ridge, and has a 12km curtain wall. The road winds steeply up through a series of seven monumental gateways. Beside them, several *chhatris* (canopied memorials) mark the sites where famous princes and heroes fell in battle.

Palace of Rana Kumbha (1433–68)

A typical Rajput complex of finely cut stuccoed stone, the palace has private and state apartments, horse and elephant stables, a *zenana* (*see p19*), and a temple to Shiva. It is said to stand on the site of Queen Padmini's *jauhar*. Nearby are the **Nau Lakha Bhandar** (Treasury), and the 1920s' **Fateh Prakash Palace**, now housing a dusty little museum.

Kumbha Shyam and Mira Bai temples

The larger of these two temples, built by Rana Kumbha in 1448, is dedicated to Vishnu in his incarnation as Varaha (the Boar). The smaller was built in 1540, in honour of Mira Bai, a mystic poetess and saint who dedicated her life to Krishna.

Vijai Stambha (1458–68)

This nine-storey, 36-m high Victory Tower, completely covered in carvings of scenes of everyday life, was built by Rana Kumbha to celebrate his victory over the Muslim rulers of Gujarat and Malwa.

Vijai Stambha, 15th-century victory tower

112km east of Udaipur on the Bundi/Kota road. Tourist Information Office: Janta Avas Grih. Tel: (01472) 41089. Fort open daily. Admission & video charges.

Chittorgarh

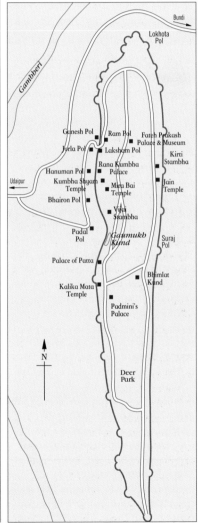

Nearby, the **Mahasati** terrace is the cremation ground of the Mewar kings.

Gaumukh Kund (Cow's Mouth)

This huge hillside reservoir is fed by a stream that gushes out from a rock that resembles a cow's mouth (*gaumukh*). It gave the fort a constant water supply, and is now a popular swimming and diving pool for local children.

Padmini's Palace

Complete with lotus pool and rose garden, this is actually a 19th-century reconstruction. Other buildings include the 12th-century **Kirti Stambha** (Tower of Fame), dedicated to Adinathji, first of the Jain *tirthankaras*, the ruined palaces of **Jaimal and Patta**, and the 8th-century **Kalika Mata Temple**, built to the sun, and converted to the worship of Kalika, patron goddess of Chittor, in the 14th century.

Hadoti Region: Bundi

In the far southeastern corner of Rajasthan, beyond the Aravalli Hills, lies the Hadoti Plateau, a fertile, well-watered land of rich black soil and highly cultivated fields. Through it flows the Chambal River, described as the Charmanyavati in the Puranas (ancient Hindu sacred texts). It is a major tributary of the Yamuna, and the only Indian river which flows south to north. Hadoti is the traditional territory of the Hada Chauhan rulers, who moved west from Mewar, conquering Bundi in 1241, and Kota in 1264.

The romance of Radha and Krishna is evoked in this miniature

The region has a wealth of fine forts and palaces, temples and villages, but has almost dropped off the tourist map; few have heard of it, even fewer make the trek to this green and peaceful area.

BUNDI

This delightful small town, named after either the *bando nal* (the twisting, steep-sided river valley in which it is situated), or *Bunda*, a 13th-century local Meena chieftain, has a lake, hills and a spectacular fort, rising steeply up the northern hillside, but sadly, in a terrible state of repair. Conquered by Rao Deva in 1241, it accepted Mughal supremacy in 1561. The town is still relatively untouched by tourism, but several of the major hotel chains are talking of opening up here – as soon as quarrels within the erstwhile royal family cease.
39km north of Kota and 206km south of Jaipur. Reached by road or, less conveniently, by rail. All Delhi–Bombay trains stop at Kota. Tourist Information Office: Circuit House. Tel: (0747) 22697.

84 Pillar cenotaph

This large memorial *chhatri* was built in 1633 in memory of Dhaibhai Dewa, foster brother of Rao Raja Anirudh Singh. It should be seen when impressively lit up at night.
About 3km south of the town centre, on the Kota road. Free admission.

Nawal Sagar

In the centre of this small, rectangular, artificial lake, built by Rao Raja Umed Singh (1739–70), is a half-submerged temple to Varuna, God of Water. The lake offers a stunning mirror reflection of the palace complex.
Below the palace. Free admission.

Fort and palace

Founded by Rao Bar Singh and finished in 1354, the hilltop **Taragarh** (Star Fort) once had walls, bastions and water tanks, and was capable of withstanding a protracted siege. Below it, the complex palace now tumbles down the hillside. The precipitous path leading up to its

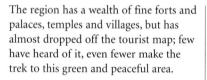

inner court passes through the **Hazari Pol** (Gate of the Thousand), home of the palace guard, and the **Hathi Pol** (Elephant Gate), beside which are the remnants of a water clock.

Bundi is famous for its miniature paintings, depicting flowers, trees, birds, the *ragas,* and Radha-Krishna legends. The **Chittra Shala**, built by Rao Raja Umed Singh (1739–70), is a colonnaded quadrangle filled with joyous depictions of court life and love scenes. More frescoes can be seen by torchlight in a room behind. Other rooms include the **Badal Mahal,** with painted ceilings of picturesque clouds (*badal*), and the

newer **Chhattar Maha**l, built in 1632, the **Ratan Daulat**, each of its pillars topped by stone elephants, and **Diwan-i-Aam**, both built by Rao Raja Rattan Singh (1607–31). Tragically, the majority of Bundi's palace paintings are now deteriorating, their decay accelerated by roosting bats.

Open: daily 8am–6pm. Upper section of the palace generally open. Free admission. To see the rest, you need permission from the maharaja himself (ask for details at the Tourist Information Office).

Raniji ki Baoli
See p87.

Little-known Bundi Fort equals the finest in Rajasthan

The international boundaries on this m
are neither purported to be correct no
authenticated by Survey of India direct

Cycle Tour: Bundi and Jait Sagar

This flat, gentle cycle ride follows a delightful lakeshore road, returning through the main bazaar. You can hire bicycles near the bus stand. The distance is about 9km. *Allow two to three hours.*

Start from the bus station. Cycle north. Take the right fork and follow the road along the town walls, past the Meera Gate, on your left, and through the terracotta Sukhi Bari Gate, to come out beside the lake. On your right is the Sukh Mahal.

Bundi lake is a haven of peace and tranquillity, far from the chaos of urban India

1 Jait Sagar
Built by Rao Raja Bhij Singh in the early-17th century, this has to be one of the prettiest lakes in Rajasthan, surrounded by steep, wooded hills. Perched on the dam wall, the charming little **Sukh Mahal** (Palace of Bliss), now known more prosaically as the Irrigation Guest House, was built in 1773 as a royal guest house. Rudyard Kipling was one of its many famous visitors.

2 Tourist bungalow and boats
A little further along on the left is a small tourist bungalow. There are boats or pedaloes for hire from the jetty below. On the hill opposite the bungalow is a little white mosque, the Meera Saheb, the 15th-century mausoleum of a Muslim chieftain who died here in battle.

3 Terraced garden
Next door, these pretty public gardens, opened in 1987 and festooned in bougainvillaea, were designed to provide entertainment for the locals. During the evenings they are brilliantly decked out in coloured lights and blasted with Hindi film music.
Keep following the road round the

lakeshore. About 2km further along, on the right, are the Kshar Bagh tombs.

4 Kshar Bagh Tombs

This overgrown and tangled garden is the old cremation ground of the Bundi royal family. Sixty-six *chhatris* huddle beneath the trees. The finest belongs to Chattar Sal Singh; the earliest is that of Kumer Duda Singh, killed in 1581.
After another 1.5km, a temple complex is reached.

5 Shikar Burj

Near the road is a small, heavily restored 11th-century temple complex. The surrounding tanks are now used as the local bathhouse. Tucked into the trees behind is an old palace built by Rao Raja Umed Singh in 1770, after his abdication in favour of his son, Ajit Singh. It later became a hunting lodge, and is now used as a school.
Cycle back round the lake, but take the right-hand fork along the narrow dirt road into the old city.

6 Old Town bazaar

There are several old temples scattered among the narrow alleys and busy market stalls of the tiny town centre, but the real reason to come here is to soak up the wonderful atmosphere.
Follow the road straight through and out of the far gate. Just beyond, beside the main road, is the Raniji ki Baoli.

7 Raniji ki Baoli

Bundi has over 50 *kunds* (tanks) and *baolis* (stepped wells). The most beautiful is the graceful, golden stone Raniji ki Baoli, built in 1699 by Rani

Nathawati, wife of Rao Raja Anirudha Singh. In theory, nothing more than a public well, it is nearly 100m long and about 12m wide, and is accessed by a steep flight of broad stairs. Above it soars a series of graceful *toran* arches decorated with friezes of marching elephants.

If feeling energetic, you can, after turning left for the bus station, carry on down the road towards the 84 Pillar Cenotaph. If not, return to your starting point.

Kshar Bagh Open: sunrise–sunset. Free admission.
Shikar Burj Free admission.
Raniji ki Baoli Free admission.

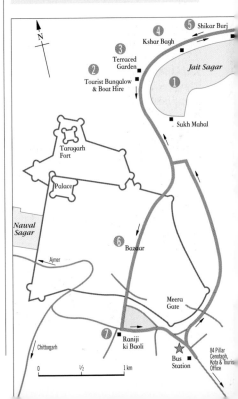

Hadoti Region: Kota

Sitting on the Chambal River, rapidly growing Kota is Rajasthan's biggest industrial city. Despite its cocktail of hydro-electric power stations, nuclear power and chemical plants, the city retains some greenery with tree-lined avenues and streets. It was ruled by the Hada Chauhans from the 13th century, a territory of Bundi traditionally held by the maharaja's eldest son. In 1641, Shah Jahan gave it to Rao Madho Singh as an independent kingdom, as a reward for gallant service.

245km south of Jaipur and 504km from Delhi, reached by road, rail or air. Tourist Information Office: Hotel Chambal, Nayapura. Tel: (0744) 327695.

Chambal Gardens

This pleasant and beautifully maintained municipal park on the banks of the Chambal is a popular picnic spot, laid out with topiary hedges, a small zoo, crocodile pens, children's playground and a toy train.
Beside Amar Niwas, Rawat Bhata Rd. Free admission. Boats for hire.

Cenotaphs

This is one of the most attractive groups of royal cenotaphs in Rajasthan. The earliest memorial dates from 1581, the latest from the 19th century. Most are in marble; all have a *Shiva lingam* (*see p21*). They are tucked under the old city's walls, originally built of mud in the 13th century by Koteya Bheel, the city founder. The walls were replaced with stone by Rao Madho Singh (r.1625–49).
Kshar Bagh Gardens, beside Kishore Sagar. Free admission.

The Fort

At the heart of the old city stands the massive fort complex, founded in 1264 by Prince Jet Singh who slew Koteya Bheel and brought the area under Chauhan rule. *Puja* is still offered daily beside Koteya's grave, near the fort gate. The massive triple wall of the fort (35

THE IMPORTANCE OF COLOUR

Colour has great significance in traditional Rajasthani dress. Only Rajput men can wear yellow turbans. Those of Brahmins are orange and yellow, while businessmen wear orange, lower castes dark red, and farmers and those in mourning, white. Younger women wear saris or richly embroidered skirts and bodices of pink, red, yellow and orange; those in black, blue, green, grey or white are widows. Saffron, the colour of purity, marks the robes worn by a *sadhu* (holy man).

to 40m high) has six double gates. The modern entrance, through the heavy **Naya Darwaza** (New Gate), leads to **Jaleb Chowk** (Big Square), a huge central courtyard which was formerly used for military parades. Just inside, the **Hawa Mahal** (Wind Palace) of 1864 is modelled on the one in Jaipur. To the left is a series of red sandstone palaces, most of them now home to schools and offices.

To the right, in the massive white palace complex, is the excellent **Rao Madho Singh Museum**, entered through the highly ornamental **Hathi Pol**, built by Rao Madho Singh. The decorative elephants were added to the structure by Maharao Bhim Singh (r.1707–20), who also added the **Durbar Hall**, covered with miniature paintings depicting the history of the palace. The many pavilions in the palace are delightful; they are decorated with marble screens, gilding, mirrorwork and crystal, while the museum exhibits paintings, furniture, photographs and armour. The miniature wall paintings are considered some of India's finest.

Rao Madho Singh Museum.
Open: 11am–5pm. Closed: Fri.
Admission & photo charge.

Jag Mandir

Lying just beyond the old city walls, the lovely Kishore Sagar lake was created in 1346 by the prince Dheer Deh of Bundi. To the north, in the Brijvilas Palace, is the **Government Museum**, behind which are a park and zoo. In the centre of the lake is an elegant three-storey red-and-white island palace, the **Jag Mandir**, built by Maharani Brij Kunwar (from Udaipur) in 1740.

Museum open: Sat–Thur 10am–5pm.
Admission charge. Permission to visit
from Superintendent Engineer, Tourist
Information Office. Tel: (0744) 327695.
Visitors can hire boats to take them
across.

The 18th-century Jag Mandir, Kota Lake

HADOTI ENVIRONS
Baroli temples (Badoli)

Built between the 8th and 12th centuries, this cluster of nine temples, dedicated to Shiva, stands on the banks of the Chambal River, surrounded by dense forest. The complex is thought to have been founded by Raja Hoon of Rhysoregarh. Some of the statues have been defaced by Aurangzeb's over-zealous Muslim armies, but most of the intricate carvings, particularly those in the main temple of Ghateshwara Mahadeo, are still wonderful, with a wealth of dancing girls and nymphs, and a superb image of Shiva as Nataraja, Lord of the Dance.

48km southwest of Kota, near the Rawatbhata nuclear power station. Free admission.

Bijolia temples

Once an important walled city ruled by the Chauhans, Bijolia was also a pilgrimage site with over 100 temples. A small village now cowers behind the walls, and only three of the stunningly beautiful 10th-century temples remain standing, surrounded by fields, their ornately sculpted towers similar to those of south India. There is a giant figure of Ganesh and an unusual three-faced image of Shiva.

48km west of Bundi, on the Chittor/ Udaipur road. Free admission.

Darrah Game Sanctuary

Covering 130sq km of woodland, the Darrah Game Sanctuary is home to a variety of wildlife, including sambar, *nilgai*, cheetal, wild boar, hyena and

The remote 10th-century Bijolia temples are among the oldest in Rajasthan

The Menal Shiva temples are all that remain of Prithviraj Chauhan's mountain stronghold

leopard. Used as a royal hunting preserve, this strategic mountain pass was earlier the site of many battles. The ruined 5th-century **Bhim Chauri temple** complex includes a stone inscription commemorating a Gupta general, Dhruvaswamy, who died here in battle against the Huns. The temple is dedicated to the *Mahabharata* hero, Bhima, who is believed to have married the demon princess Hidimba here.
58km southwest of Kota, on NH12 to Jhalawar. Contact the Forestry Department for permission to enter and to hire a jeep.

Jhalawar

A small and almost totally unknown princely state, Jhalawar was carved off from Kota in 1838. The city itself has a fort, now used as offices, with some fine paintings, and a good government museum. The **Bhawani Natya Shala** was used for theatre, and has recently been restored. In the 19th century, the historian, James Todd, counted 108 temples in nearby **Jhalarapatan** (City of Temple Bells). Still magnificent are the 10th-century **Surya temple**, 11th-century **Shantinath Jain temple**, and the group of 6th- to 14th-century **Chandramauleshwar temples**. Also nearby is the formidable 8th- to 14th-century **Gagron Fort**. Its useful life came to an end when conquered by Akbar in 1561.
85km southeast of Kota on NH12.

Menal Shiva temples

After his defeat by Mohammed Ghori in 1192, Prithviraj Chauhan, the last Rajput ruler of Delhi, retreated to this mountain haven. Only a few stones mark his former palaces, but there are still several fine 12th-century Shiva temples beside the Menal River gorge. There is a really good waterfall during the monsoon.
64km west of Bundi, on the Chittor/ Udaipur road. Free admission.

Ramgarh

This complex of Shiva temples was carved from the hillside in the 10th century under the auspices of Raja Malay Varman. The main temple, 49m long, 32m wide and 32m high, was created from a single rock. The carvings of gods and goddesses outside, and the erotic figures inside, are slightly later, and not so fine as the famous Khajuraho figures. The whole complex is deteriorating fast.
110km east of Kota. Free admission.

Jaipur

Jaipur (City of Victory) was built by Maharaja Jai Singh II (1700–1743), ruler of Amber (*see p98*), and a true Renaissance man. At the young age of 11, he so impressed Emperor Aurangzeb that he was awarded the title 'Sawai' (literally 'one and a quarter'). Thereafter, all the Jaipur rulers were given this title. In 1727 he and his Bengali architect, Vidhya Chakravarty, laid out a new city, capital of the Kachhwaha clan, and centre of one of the three most powerful and splendid states of Rajasthan.

One of the grand gateways to Chokri Sarhad (City Palace) in Jaipur

The city plan followed the classic Hindu treatise of architecture, the *Shilpa-Shastra*. Based on the nine cosmic divisions of the universe, it had a grid of nine blocks, and a planned hierarchy of roads. Local aristocracy and merchants were invited to settle, and built handsome *havelis* (courtyard-style houses), temples and wells, all of which followed an overall grand design.

Jaipur became capital of all Rajasthan in 1956. It is now a thriving centre with a population of about 2 million. The city has a laid-back atmosphere, and the historic 'pink city' remains intact, one of the architectural glories of the world. Several city palaces are now hotels (*see pp172–5*).

259km from Delhi, with good road, rail and air connections. RTDC Tourist Office: Hotel Swagatam Campus, near railway station, M1 Rd. Tel: (0141) 2202761; Rajasthan Government Information Bureau: railway station. Tel: (0141) 2315714; Tourist Information Office: Hotel Khasa Kothi, MI Rd. Tel: (0141) 2372200.

Central Museum (Albert Hall)

This ornate Indo-Saracenic confection was built by British architect, Sir Samuel Swinton Jacob, to commemorate the visit of the Prince of Wales in 1876. Although somewhat dusty, the museum has some superb carpets, ivory carvings, inlay and brasswork, and a 30-m long *phad* (painted scroll on the life of Pabuji, a folk hero of Rajasthan). *Ram Niwas Gardens. Tel: (0141) 2565124. Open: 10am–4.30pm. Closed: Fri. Admission charge.*

Chokri Sarhad (City Palace)

This huge complex, built at the same time as the city, has a wealth of internal furnishings and art. The ex-maharaja still lives in part of the palace.

The **Mubarak Mahal** (Textiles and Costumes Gallery) – the ivory-like pavilion in the main courtyard – now houses a wonderful exhibition of musical instruments, textiles and clothes, including the awe-inspiringly large tunic and trousers of Maharaja Madho Singh I (r.1750–1768), who was reputed to be 2m tall, weigh 270kg, and have fathered 100 children. Behind the Mubarak Mahal is the **Sileh Khana** (Armoury). Diamond and gold encrusted pistols, daggers and helmets, and a lethal steel mace are part of its superb collection. 'Welcome' in knives and 'Goodbye' in pistols are spelt out above the doors.

Flanked by marble elephants, the **Rajendra Pol** leads through to the **Diwan-i-Khas** (Hall of Private Audience). Two urns are the largest silver items in the world, with a capacity of 9,000 litres (they are listed in the *Guinness Book of Records*). They were commissioned by Madho Singh II to carry sacred Ganges water for his visit to London in 1902.

To the left, the **Riddhi Siddhi Pol** leads through into the **Pritam Chowk** (Court of the Beloved), with four enchanting **Peacock Doorways**, each representing a season. The rooms beyond contain fine Mughal glass.

On the opposite side of the complex, the enclosed **Diwan-i-Aam** (Hall of Public Audience) now houses the **Art Gallery**, with a fabulous array of carpets, miniature paintings, and around 20,000 manuscripts.
Off Tripolia and Sireh Deori Bazaar. Tel: (0141) 2608055. Open: daily 9.30am–4.45pm. Admission & photo charge. Keep ticket for use in every section. Ram Singh II's collection of black and white photographs can be seen in the Diwan-i-Aam with permission.

Each of the elephants flanking Rajendra Pol is made from a single block of marble

The Hawa Mahal, five storeys high, one room deep and open to the wind

Govindji temple
See p98.

Hawa Mahal (Palace of the Winds)
Five storeys tall, but only one room deep, this delightful building was constructed in 1799 for the ladies of the *zenana* to observe the outside world unseen. Its name derives from the constant cool breeze that blows through the latticed screens on its 953 windows. On the ground floor are a small art gallery and a museum of Jaipuri history. The shops opposite hire their balconies and roofs to those who want a better photographic angle of what is actually the rear face of Hawa Mahal.
Sireh Deori Bazaar (entrance from west). Open: daily 9am–4.30pm. Admission & photo charge.

Jantar Mantar
See pp98–9.

Lakshmi Narayan temple (Birla Temple)
Built by the industrialist Birla family in 1979, this gleaming white marble temple is named after the goddess of wealth. Built on the old fort of Shakargarh, the **Moti Doongri** fort above, with its Scottish turrets, is a private royal property, closed to visitors.
Jawaharlal Nehru Marg. Free admission.

Jaipur City

Museum of Indology

This private collection is an eccentric mix of ancient manuscripts, textiles, tantric art and oddities such as Hindi script painted on a hair.

Prachya Vidya Path, 24 Gangwal Park. Tel: (0141) 2607455. Open: daily 10am–5pm. Admission charge.

Nahargarh Fort (Tiger Fort)

Perched dramatically on a cliff, this fort, built in 1734, and extended in the 19th century, was designed to protect Jaipur and house the city treasure. The view from its ramparts is magnificent.

Above the city; access off the Amber road, or up a steep footpath. Tel: (0141) 2671848. Open: daily 9am–4.30pm. Admission & photo charge. Restaurant and café open all evening.

Rambagh Palace

See p168.

Note: Map numbers refer to Pink City Walk *on page 98.*

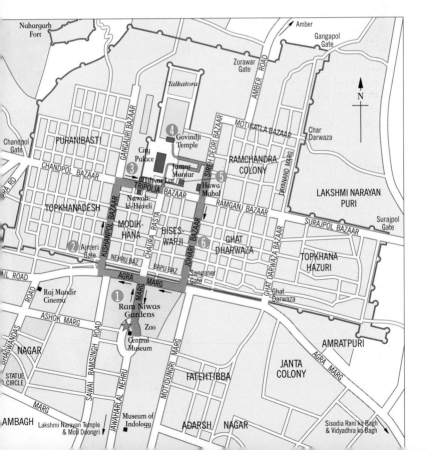

Mystery surrounds the origins of the Rajputs, who seem to have sprung, fully armed, from the desert sands in about the 8th century AD. They claim direct Aryan descent back to the sun, moon and fire. More probably, they were warlike pre-Aryan natives, Hun and Scythian invaders (6th–7th centuries) who received *kshatriya* (warrior/ruler) caste status in a ritual purification by fire. Whatever the case, for the last 1,000 years, they have ruled Rajasthan with an iron grip.

There are 36 clans, the most prominent being: Kachhwaha (Amber/Jaipur), Rathore (Bikaner/Jodhpur), Sisodia (Udaipur), Bhatti (Jaisalmer), Chauhan (Ajmer) and Hada Chauhan (Bundi/Kota). All the men, whether ruler of a single village or a great state, take the title Singh (Lord).

The Rajputs (literally, son of a king), gradually carved themselves kingdoms in a welter of blood, building up a splendid

legendary tradition of romance, chivalry and extravagant valour, still very much alive today. In reality, many rulers were more pragmatic. Only one, Maharana Pratap Singh of Udaipur, refused to submit to the Mughals, while the others struck deals, and even intermarried.

Hindu and Muslim cultures borrowed freely from each other, and most of the great forts and palaces have Mughal features. The Rajputs even adopted the Islamic tradition of *purdah*, adding it to the Vedic practice of *sati* – both examples of the feudal culture of their society. Their greatest heroine, Queen Padmini (*see p82*), led her court in *jauhar* (self immolation) rather than let her face be seen by a lascivious invader, while the men donned saffron and went out to fight a last suicidal battle.

The rulers have since been dethroned, but many still live in palaces; some have entered politics, and others are captains of industry (in Rajasthan, over 70 per cent of the tourist trade is in Rajput hands). Deeply conservative, they dream of past glories, still wield immense authority – particularly in rural communities – and are determined to hang on to their traditional, if not their legal status.

Clockwise from left: *sati* prints in Bikaner mark the princesses who burnt on their husbands' funeral pyres; Rajputs are keen hunters as well as warriors; royal cenotaphs in Jaisalmer; ex-Maharaja Surendra Singh at home in Shahpura

Walk: Pink City

This gentle walk takes in the best of the walled city, including the City Palace, and the shopping bazaars. For highlights along the route, see the Jaipur city map on pages 94–5.

Allow about one hour walking, plus sightseeing and shopping time.

The international boundaries on this m are neither purported to be correct no authenticated by Survey of India direct

Start in the Ram Niwas Gardens.

1 Ram Niwas Gardens

These popular gardens were laid out by the last maharaja, Man Singh II (1922–49), as a famine relief project. At the centre is the splendid Central Museum (*see p92*), and nearby are a small zoo and a bird park – good on atmosphere, but short on animals.
Walk up towards the old town, turn left along Agra Marg, and right through the Ajmeri Gate.

2 City walls and gates

The imposing city wall with its seven monumental gates is for effect as much as for defence. The Tripolia Gate leads into the city palace. The city is built of natural greyish-pink sandstone, but its current, rather startling colour dates back to 1876 when the extravagant Maharaja Ram Singh II painted the entire town to welcome the Prince of Wales (pink is the Rajasthani colour of hospitality).
Walk up Kishanpol Bazaar, and turn right into Tripolia Bazaar. On your right, Nawab Saheb ki Haveli is one of the finest merchants' houses in the city. As you proceed, on your left is a white tower.

3 Ishvar Lat

This tower, the 'minaret which pierces the heavens', was built by Raja Sawai Ishwari Singh in 1749 in order to commemorate his victory over his step-brother, Madho Singh I.
Further on, to your left, are two gateways into the palace complex.
Use the smaller Atish Gate, but first have a quick look at the magnificent main Tripolia Gate, opened only for ceremonial processions. For the City Palace, see pp92–3.

4 Govindji Temple

Just north of the palace, this temple was built to house an image of Govind (Krishna as a cowherd) – one of the Jaipur family's presiding deities – rescued from Mathura and the advancing Mughals.

The temple was designed so that the maharaja could view the image from his terraces. There are seven ceremonies honouring the idol each day (5am–9pm).

5 Jantar Mantar

South (right) of the main palace entrance is the Jantar Mantar (literally 'Instrument to Make Calculations').

Built between 1728 and 1734, this is the largest, most ambitious, and best preserved of five astronomical observatories constructed by Jai Singh II, who was fascinated by science and became a world-class astronomer. It has 18 different instruments, used to plot the movement of the sun, stars and moon, and calculate time, date, the expected date of arrival, duration and intensity of the monsoon, and the signs of the zodiac.

Leave the complex by the gate on to Sireh Deori Bazaar. Turn right, and almost immediately on your right is the Hawa Mahal (see p94). Cross straight over at the crossroads and walk down through Johari Bazaar.

6 Johari Bazaar

A broad street which is seemingly crammed 24 hours a day with people and shops, vehicular traffic and camel carts, this is the most interesting of Jaipur's bazaars. Shops on both the main street and the myriad side alleys specialise in textiles and gold jewellery. *At the far end, Sanganer Gate leads back through the city walls. Get a rickshaw from here, or turn right for the museum.*

Ram Niwas Gardens *Open: Mar–Oct, daily 8am–6pm; Oct–Mar, daily 8am–5.30pm. Closed: Tue. Admission charge.*
Ishvar Lat is closed to the public.
Jantar Mantar *Open: Sat–Thu 10am–4.30pm. Admission & photo charge.*

Vegetable and fruit street vendors vie for space in front of a temple (marked by a red signpost)

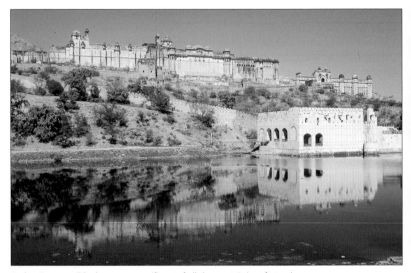

Amber Fort, possibly the most magnificent of all the great Rajput fort-palaces

JAIPUR ENVIRONS
Amber Fort

The name is romantic (pronounced without the b), but the reality of this vast, magnificent fortified palace is far more so. Built in 1592 by Maharaja Man Singh I, it was by no means the first fort on the site. The Kachhwaha family had reigned here since the 11th century, and the surrounding hills are littered with ruins of older forts and the settlement below. Perilously near Agra, the family became the first of the Rajput rulers to agree terms with the Mughals. Bihar Mal (1548–74) married his daughter, Jodhabai, to Akbar, and his adopted grandson, Man Singh, was a renowned general in Akbar's army. In return, the family reaped honours, influence and rewards. The design of Amber Fort is strongly influenced by the decorative elements of Mughal architecture.

Views of Amber

On rounding the corner of the steep valley road from Jaipur, a magnificent view of the fort is seen, carved into the hillside, and reflected in the waters of **Moata Lake**, in front, with the brooding bulk of **Jaigarh Fort** (*see p103*) hovering in the distance, and its formidable defensive walls marching off across the heights. Behind the lake, a steep twisting path winds up past the formal terraced **Dil-e-Aaram Gardens** to the monumental entrance, **Suraj Pol** (Sun Gate).

Outer courtyards

The first court, the **Jaleb Chowk**, originally the parade ground, is filled with souvenir shops and decorated elephants. Further in, almost out of sight, beside the stairs, is the **Shila Devi Temple** – the family shrine dedicated to Kali, goddess of war, whose 16th-century image was brought from Bengal in east India to be installed here in fulfilment of a vow.

The **Singh Pol** (Lion Gate) leads into the first royal court and the **Diwan-i-Aam** (Hall of Public Audience), with a red sandstone canopy surrounded by carved elephants and delicately decorated walls, said to be so beautiful that they were covered in stucco to appease the envious Mughal emperor Jahangir. The terrace is a favourite hangout for monkeys. Beyond this is the vivid **Ganesh Pol** (Elephant Gate), built by Jai Singh I in 1640. It is a riot of mosaic, fresco, sculpture and colour.

Private apartments

The third courtyard is filled with flowers in season. To the right is the **Sukh Niwas** (Hall of Pleasure), cooled by running water and fountains. To the left, the marble **Jai Mandir** (Temple of Victory) acted as the **Diwan-i-Khas** (Hall of Private Audience). Behind it lies Amber's greatest treasure, the **Sheesh Mahal** (Hall of Mirrors), a series of truly fabulous, glittering rooms patterned all over with mirrors and niches for oil lamps. These formed part of the maharaja's private apartments. Upstairs, the little **Jas Mahal,** also known as Jas Mandir, has a superb lacy marble screen, and offers wonderful views down the valley. Beyond this courtyard, the oldest part of the palace is in poor repair.

11km north from Jaipur, on the Delhi Road. Tel: (0141) 2530293. Open: daily 9am–4.30pm. Admission & photo charge. It is a steep climb up from the car park. Walk or hire a jeep or an elephant.

Gaitor
See p102.

Sisodia Rani ka Bagh
Built by Maharaja Jai Singh II in 1710 for his wife, Sisodia Rani of Udaipur, who wished to live away from court, this delicately decorated little palace, one of the prettiest in Rajasthan, is sadly closed and can be seen only from the outside. Its formal gardens, once alive with dancing peacocks and gurgling fountains, are barely maintained.
8km from Jaipur on the Agra road. Open: gardens 8am–6pm. Admission charge.

Vidyadhar ka Bagh
Named after Jai Singh's architect who is believed to have planned Jaipur, this is another sad remnant of what must have been a delightful garden in the formal Mughal style.
Opposite the Sisodia palace, 8km east of Jaipur on the Agra road. Open: daily 8am–6pm. Admission charge.

The fabulous Hall of Mirrors gleams like stars

Tour: Jaipur to Amber

This is the classic tour done by all visitors, linking the two great cities, modern Jaipur and historic Amber.

Allow a very long morning to do it justice.

The international boundaries on this r are neither purported to be correct nc authenticated by Survey of India direc

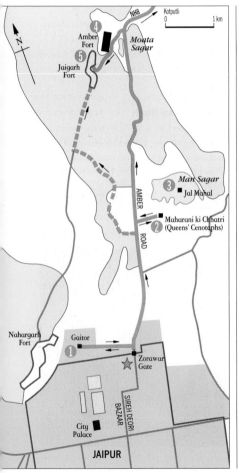

Leave the walled city of Jaipur by Zorawar Gate. Shortly afterwards, a road to the left leads off to Gaitor (about 1km)

1 Gaitor (Royal cenotaphs)

Tucked beneath Nahargarh Fort is the cremation ground of all the Jaipur rulers (except Sawai Ishwari Singh), dedicated to the ruling Sun God of the Kachhwaha family. Many of the individual cenotaphs are beautiful, with delicately sculpted friezes and columns. The finest is the 20-pillared mausoleum of Jai Singh II (1743), carved with Hindu mythological scenes. Others of note include Madho Singh I (1768), Pratap Singh (1803), and Sawai Ram Singh II (1880).

Return to the main road and turn left, continuing towards Amber. There are numerous factory shops along this road, making and selling carpets, Jaipur pottery, blockprint and other fabrics (see pp154–5). After about 2km, on your right, are the queens' cenotaphs.

2 Maharani ki Chhatri

This is the cremation ground of the royal wives and children. While none of the mausoleums are as magnificent as those of the kings, the carvings here too have a wonderful quality.

A short way beyond is a small lake, nearly drowned by a sea of water hyacinth.

3 Jal Mahal

This now inaccessible palace in the centre of the Man Sagar (lake) seems impossibly romantic, but was actually an overgrown shooting hide built by Sawai Madho Singh I for hunting parties.
The road now winds steeply through a mountain pass to the Amber Fort. From the car park, walk or, more easily, but expensively, take an elephant.

4 Amber Fort

See p100.

Dizzyingly perched above Amber is Jaigarh Fort. An almost vertical 1.5km path links the two. To reach it by road, backtrack towards Jaipur; after you pass the Jal Mahal, a road to the right leads up the mountain. At the top the road forks; turn right for Jaigarh, or left for Nahargarh Fort (see p95).

5 Jaigarh Fort

This magnificent mountain stronghold dates back to the 11th century, but was rebuilt by Jai Singh II in 1726, some say, as a home for royal treasure. The taxmen hunted for six months in 1976 before concluding that the treasure was gone. The fort was used as a gun foundry from 1584 onwards. Its decorative Jai Vana cannon, cast in 1726, and claimed to be the largest in the world, has only been fired once, as a test, when the ball travelled 38km. The museum has a fine collection of arms, many of them made here, displayed with histories of where they were used. The palace complex behind includes a couple of small temples and a puppet theatre.
Return to the main road to reach Jaipur.

Jaigarh Fort *Open: daily 9am–4.30pm. Admission & vehicle charges.*
Cenotaphs *Open: from sunrise to sunset. Free admission.*

The now flooded Jal Mahal was once a hunting lodge

Jaisalmer

A magnificent citadel rising from Trikuta Hill like a gold crown above the desert plain, Jaisalmer is one of the oldest Rajasthani forts. It was built in 1156 when Prince Jaisal, officially regent to his nephew, seized power for himself and moved the capital from nearby, more vulnerable Lodurva, to this huge defensive fortress. The hermit who showed him the spot prophesied, rightly, that the fort would be sacked two and a half times.

Looking out over the ramparts of Jaisalmer Fort

The early ruling Bhatti family behaved like bandits, looting and rustling at will. Attacks on Jaisalmer between the early-14th and 16th centuries by Muslim invaders and rulers came in retaliation for Bhatti raids, resulting in defeat and large-scale *jauhar* by the inhabitants. Finally, a matrimonial alliance in 1570 between the ruling family and Emperor Akbar ensured peace. For the next two

Jaisalmer Fort soars above the desert, crowning Trikuta Hill

centuries, the town prospered as a trade centre on camel caravan routes to the Middle East, attracting hard-working Paliwal Brahmins and Jains, who invested heavily in building beautifully carved *havelis* and temples. New arrivals were given one rupee, one stone and one day's labour to help them get started, and the town grew rich. In the late-18th century, however, this situation was to change.

First the trade collapsed as the sea trade grew; then the notoriously cruel prime minister, Salim Singh Mehta (1784–1824), imposed taxes instead of voluntary donations and, even more heinously, tried to marry a Brahmin girl. The Brahmins scattered, taking their wealth and cursing the town, prophesying that the monsoon would vanish forever. By the end of the century, the population had dropped drastically, and there was terrible drought. The final blow was the

Partition, which established a border between India and Pakistan, cutting off the old existing, overland trade routes.

In 1965, India and Pakistan went to war, and strategically important Jaisalmer gained a road and an air force base. In 1975, Indira Gandhi visited the base and earmarked the crumbling town for tourist development. Today, it has a railway, and three flights a week from Delhi via Jodhpur. Tourism remains the main source of revenue despite its often adverse visible effects such as burgeoning signboards. Jaisalmer is unlike any other Rajput city, a vision of gold as it rises from the desert to be justly known as the Golden City.
275km west of Jodhpur, reached by road, rail, and air. Rajasthan Tourism Office: Tel: (02992) 52406.

Note: Map numbers refer to Walk *on pages 110–11.*

Jaisalmer

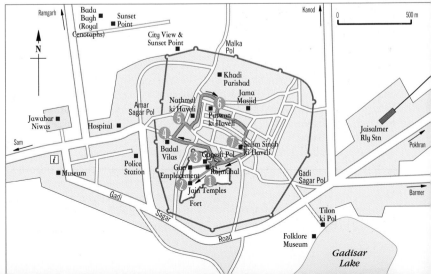

Bada Bagh

The royal cremation grounds are set between the desert and a rain-fed lake, where a wheat crop is planted each year as the lake dries up. Each of the cenotaphs has a central column with a bas relief of its owner. Many are accompanied by figures for wives or consorts who committed *sati* on his funeral pyre. You can see a definite progression of style from the trabeate construction of the early Hindu monuments at the back to the cusped arches of later, Mughal-influenced architecture. Bada Bagh is a particularly good point from which to view the sunset.

About 6km north of Jaisalmer, off the Ramgarh road. Admission & photo charge.

Citadel

Typical of the great fort settlements of northern India, Jaisalmer's citadel, surrounded by an inner defensive wall, dominates the settlement on its northern side. The settlement had its own protective wall (much of it now broken). Built entirely without mortar, this 12th- to 16th-century yellow sandstone fort sits atop a hill, while steep cliffs tumble beneath the 99 bastions to the plain. Of four entrances, only one is still used. This is the only Indian fort where people still live and own property – almost 8,000 dwell in houses densely packed together, some of which are exquisitely decorated.

Gates

There are several successive monumental gateways. **Ganesh Pol**, dedicated to the Elephant God, is followed by the **Suraj Pol** (Sun Gate). Just beyond is the **Signal Balcony** on the right, traditionally used to play drums as a warning of approaching visitors. It was last used as an air-raid warning during the Indo-Pakistan Wars (1965 and 1971). Beyond this are the **Bhooth Pol** (Haunted Gate), with a temple dedicated to the warlike Bhatti ruling goddess, Bhavani, and the cool and breezy **Hawa Pol** (Wind Gate).

City Palace

As you enter the citadel, the main *chowk* is where ceremonial sacrifice and *jauhar* were performed, and the king reviewed his troops or gave public audience. Beside it, several small 14th- to 19th-century buildings make up the now empty and crumbling **Raj Mahal** or maharaja's palace. Some of the rooms still retain their beautiful decorations, with tiles of roses, miniature paintings, and lacy marble screens. Look in particular for the paintings of 18th-century Jaisalmer.

Jain temples

At the heart of the citadel stands a group of seven interconnecting Jain temples, built between 1470 and 1536 by wealthy traders. Their generosity created magnificent works of art. This includes intricate chandeliers carved from a single stone, elaborate *toran* arches of welcome, and pillars and domes covered with a chattering mass of sculpted girls. Round the walls are friezes of elephants, chariots and Hindu deities, created in gratitude for the religious tolerance of the maharawals (local rulers). The cross-legged statues of the *tirthankaras* seem

Seven interconnecting Jain temples lie at the heart of the citadel

austere in their comparative simplicity. Below the third temple is an important library containing precious palm leaf and other manuscripts dating back to the 11th century, a statue of Mahavira (the founder of Jainism) made of emeralds, and a copy of the Lodurva Tree of Imagination (*see pp108–9*).
Free access to the Citadel at all times. Raj Mahal, Dashara Chowk open: daily 8am–1pm & 3–5pm. Admission charge. Jain temples open: daily 8am–noon; library 10am–11am only. Free admission but photo charge. Leather shoes not permitted.

Gadisar Lake
This rainwater-fed reservoir, southeast of the city walls, was built in 1156, and rebuilt in 1367 by Maharawal Garsi Singh. Until 1965, it remained the city's only water supply (now supplied by pipe from the Indira Gandhi Canal). The **Tilon ki Pol**, the palatial archway at the water's edge, was built by a famous local courtesan. The horrified king tried to tear it down but, staying one jump ahead, Tilon added a tiny temple to Satyanarayan (Krishna, as God of Truth), and ensured that the building would survive. Along the lake shore and on the islands are a host of little temples and *chhatris.*

Folklore Museum
This delightful and informative craft museum comprises the personal collection of its owner, NK Sharma, who founded it in 1984. Eclectic displays include textiles, local geology, royal ceremony, musical instruments, coins, stamps and letters, puppets and *kavads* (box theatres).
Free access to the lake (best in early morning). Boats for hire. The Folklore Museum is open: daily 9am–noon & 3–6pm. Admission & photo charge.

For other sights in Jaisalmer, see Jaisalmer Town Walk, *pp110–11.*

Cowdung cakes drying for use as fuel

JAISALMER ENVIRONS
Amar Sagar

Northwest of Jaisalmer, this small group of buildings was once a garden and pleasure palace, and rainwater reservoir built in 1740 in honour of Maharawal Amar Singh (r.1698–1710). There are also several small temples and memorial *chhatris*. The late 17th-century complex of three Jain temples was badly damaged by monsoon floods and has since been rebuilt – the donors' names are listed on the walls.
7km northwest of Jaisalmer on the Lodurva road. Free admission for Indians, but photo charge.

Baisakhi Temple

Built in the 10th century, and rebuilt in the 16th, this Shiva temple with a deep *baoli* (stepped pond), considered to have sacred properties, is a popular place of pilgrimage. Within the grounds are several memorial pillars – records of

building work, donations and so on, and a number of shrines to Hanuman, the monkey god and giver of power.
15km north of Jaisalmer, off the Ramgarh road. Free admission.

Desert National Park
Akal Wood Fossil Park

This area was once heavily wooded with non-flowering trees such as *chir* (pine) and deodar. About 180 million years ago (during the Mesozoic era), the sea inundated the area, and on retreating again about 36 million years ago, it left behind a fossilised forest. Covering about 10sq km of bare hillside, the fossil park contains 25 fascinating petrified trunks – the largest measuring 13m long.

Sam Dunes

This small 3-km long stretch of billowing dunes is the only one easily accessible from Jaisalmer and, as such, is usually overrun by tourists on camel rides (*see p146*). It is possible to ride away from the pack, or stay out to eat or sleep under the moon, and feel the real magic of the desert sands.
30km west of Jaisalmer (285km from Jodhpur). Free admission to Akal Wood Fossil Park (20km from Jaisalmer on NH15 to Barmer) and Sam Dunes (42km west of Jaisalmer). See also p142.

Lodurva

Although this is the site of the first capital of the region, abandoned in the 12th century (*see p104*), there are few early ruins, and the main sight here is a wonderful Jain temple, built by Tharusha Bhansali around AD 1615, and shaped like a series of Chinese lanterns

fanning out from the central portico. The *toran* (entrance arch) is from an earlier temple, destroyed by Mohammed Ghori in the 12th century. The statue, made of touchstone (used to test the purity of gold) was made in Gujarat in the 17th century. On a column in the courtyard is a fantastic tree of wood and iron, the **Kalp Vrkasha** (Tree of Imagination). Made about 150 years ago, it is said to grant wishes to those who pray here. Stay alert as there are rats and a cobra living in the courtyard. *16km northwest of Jaisalmer.*
Open: daily 8am–8pm. Free admission, but photo charge.

Villages

During the rule of the greedy 18th-century prime minister, Salim Singh Mehta, the Paliwan Brahmins abandoned 84 villages surrounding Jaisalmer in order to escape taxes. Some of them have been resettled, although by other castes or army camp followers. Others are derelict, fascinating ghost towns. **Kuldhera** has been preserved as a monument to the old Brahmin communities. Nearby **Damodra** has been reoccupied, and the local children are keen to show you around. **Kanoi** is now home to communities of wood-carvers and musicians.
Damodra is 15km from Jaisalmer, 20km from Kuldhera and 37km from Kanoi, all on the road to the Sam Dunes. Most tour operators run village tours. Free admission, but baksheesh *expected.*

Camels are the lifeblood of the desert villagers

Walk: Jaisalmer Town

The international boundaries on this m
are neither purported to be correct no
authenticated by Survey of India direct

This walk provides the best possible way to
see Jaisalmer, meandering through narrow lanes, past the
intricately carved and painted doorways of the great
citadel, the crowded markets and grandiose *havelis* of
19th-century merchants in the new town. For the route,
see the Jaisalmer town map on page 105.

Allow about one hour, plus browsing and sightseeing time.

*Start in the market place, Gopa Chowk,
beside the Ganesh Pol (gate), and walk up
through the citadel.*

1 Citadel
For the Citadel *and* Raj Mahal, *see p106.*

*From Gopa Chowk, take the lane to the
right, signed Hotel Paradise, and follow it
past the hotel to the Jain temples (if in
doubt, follow the postcard stalls).*

2 Jain temples
See pp106–7.
*Turn back along the lane and then go left,
past the small Hindu temple of Lakshmi
Nath. Beyond this, scramble up the stone
stairway on to the bastion.*

3 Gun emplacements
Several of the city's old cannons still
remain on the bastions. The real reason
for coming up here, however, is for the
superb view, which seems to stretch into
forever, while eagles and kites wheel on
thermals beneath the walls.
*Return to the Gopa Chowk and leave the
fort. Turn left at the last gate, along the
line of the walls, and walk through to the*

*Amar Sagar Pol (gate), one of the few
remaining vestiges of the old town walls.
On your right is the Badal Vilas.*

4 Badal Vilas
Current home of the royal family, the
palace was built during the reign of
Maharawal Jawahar Singh (1914–46).
The five-storey tower was built as a
present to the royal family by Muslim
stone craftsmen before they emigrated
to Pakistan during Partition in 1947. It
looks like a *tazia* (model of Shia Muslim
mausoleum, made to honour the deaths
of the Prophet's grandsons). There are
numerous temples, and some massive
cooking pots in the grounds.

5 Nathmal ki Haveli
In 1886, the Maharawal Beri Sal Singh
gave this magnificent *haveli* to his prime
minister, Diwan Nathmal. It was carved
by two Muslim brothers, Hati and Laloo,
who each designed a wing. Each of the
seven balconies on the façade is carved
from a single block of stone. The
splendid stone elephants signify the
residence of a prime minister.
Continue past the haveli, *turn right and*

then right again along Noidani Mohalla, and you will come out beside the Patwon ki Haveli.

6 Patwon ki Haveli

Probably the most magnificent of all, this is actually a group of five *havelis* built in the mid-19th century by the enormously wealthy Jain businessman, Guman Chand Patwa, for his five sons. The intensely ornamented façade is quite superb, but immensely difficult to photograph. Inside, decorative rooms surround a balconied courtyard of glowing golden stone.
Walk through the bazaar in the courtyard along Acharya Mohalla, and turn right to reach the third great haveli.

7 Salim Singh ki Haveli

This extraordinary building has five relatively simple storeys, and an ornate sixth overhanging the tower. Two more were broken down in order to build a bridge to the fort by the owner, the notorious prime minister, Salim Singh, who almost destroyed the city (*see also p105*) before he was himself murdered. *From here, it is a short walk straight up the road to the Fort Gate.*

Badal Vilas Beside Amar Sagar Gate. *Tel: (02992) 52788.* Open access to courtyard only. A few rooms are run as a hotel.
Havelis Open: 10.30am–5pm. All of them have shops inside. Admission charge for **Patwon ki Haveli**.

The superb façade of Patwon ki Haveli is typical of Jaisalmer's ornate mansions

Jodhpur

Jodhpur was one of the greatest of the Rajput kingdoms, covering a massive 93,240sq km. The Rathore royal family claims descent from the great central Indian Rashtrakuta dynasty (8th–10th centuries), and through them, to the Sun. On the dynasty's decline, some people migrated north, then west. Finally, in 1192, Rao Siha moved into the Thar Desert, and in 1381, Rao Chunda conquered Mandore, 8km north of Jodhpur. The desert kingdom of Marwar (Land of Death) and the modern Rathore dynasty were born.

The towering ramparts of Meherangarh Fort

Chunda's son, Ranmal, turned his attentions to green and pleasant Mewar (Udaipur region), but failed, and was drugged and killed during a state banquet. His son, Rao Jodha (1453–89), fled back to Marwar, and shifted the capital from Mandore to the safer clifftop Jodhpur to build the massive Meherangarh Fort. In the late-16th century, the Rathores made peace with Akbar, and were awarded the title of Raja. Like other willing subjects, they flourished under Mughal protection, although it caused repercussions when Jaswant Singh, a later ruler, picked the wrong side during Aurangzeb's battle with his father, Shah Jahan, and his brother, Dara Shukoh, in a war of succession in 1658.

Jodhpur was a staging post for camel caravans linking China and the Middle East. The city grew rich on trade in silks

View over Jodhpur's Brahmin district

Jodhpur

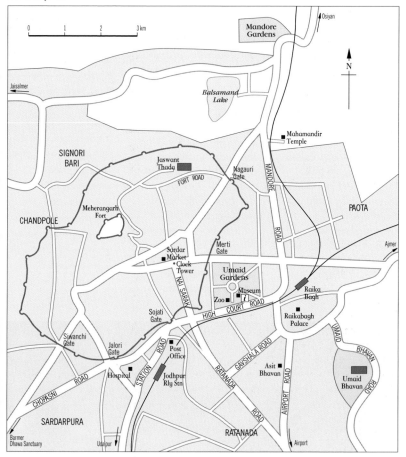

0   1   2   3 km

Osiyan

Mandore
Gardens

N

Jaisalmer

Balsamand
Lake

Mahamandir
Temple

SIGNORI
BARI

Jaswant
Thada

Nagauri
Gate

FORT ROAD

MANDORE

Meherangarh
Fort

CHANDPOLE

PAOTA

ROAD

Merti
Gate

Ajmer

Sardar
Market

Clock
Tower

Umaid
Gardens

Museum
i

Zoo

Raika
Bagh

NAI SARAK

HIGH   COURT   ROAD

Sojati
Gate

Raikabagh
Palace

UMAID

Siwanchi
Gate

Jalori
Gate

ROAD

Post
Office

GAVSHALA ROAD

BHAVAN

Asit
Bhavan

AIRPORT ROAD

Umaid
Bhavan

ROAD

CHOPSNI   ROAD

Hospital

STATION   ROAD

Jodhpur
Rly Stn

RATANADA   ROAD

SARDARPURA

Barmer
Dhawa Sanctuary

Udaipur

RATANADA

Airport

and opium, copper and coffee, sandalwood and spice, until the arrival of the British, with their merchant fleets, trade barriers, and European goods created a new maritime market. Jodhpur and Britain signed a treaty in 1818, and the canny Marwari merchants followed the trade, fanning out across India, and setting up some of India's greatest industrial powerhouses. Little of their commercial influence can be seen in Jodhpur, but they retain links with their old homes. The city population is heading for a million, but it feels like a smaller town, albeit with many facilities. *343km west of Jaipur and 602km from Delhi, with road, rail and air connections. Tourist Information Office: Hotel Ghoomar, High Court Rd. Tel: (0291) 245083/244010.*

JODHPUR RIDERS

Jodhpur is most famous for its baggy riding trousers, introduced to the British cavalry during World War I by Maharaja Pratap Singh, when he was commander of the Mounted Lancers Regiment. Later, on a sea voyage to England, he lost his luggage, and on arriving there he gave the tailor explicit instructions on how to make his trousers. The tailor needed a name to put in the order book. 'Jodhpuri', replied the maharaja – and thus a fashion was born.

Jaswant Thada

Just outside the fort is the modern royal cremation ground, centred on a huge marble monument (constructed in 1899) commemorating Maharaja Jaswant Singh II (r.1878–1895), a benevolent man who constructed schools and hospitals, roads and railways, and is considered by most to be Jodhpur's finest ruler.
Opposite Meherangarh Fort, halfway up the hill. Open: daily 10am–1pm, 2–5pm. Admission charge.

Meherangarh Fort

Founded in 1459 by Rao Jodha, this is one of the most dramatic fort-palaces in Rajasthan – a towering citadel, high on a craggy 125-m high hill, with powerful walls 10km all round and up to 45m high in places. As you walk up the steep, twisting path – designed to halt a charging elephant – through the seven monumental gateways, sheer cliffs of natural rock and smooth, blood-red local sandstone soar to a frothy summit of lacy palace balconies. Several gateways are marked by memorials to

One of the sumptuous rooms at the Meherangarh Fort

A daily market springs to life around the English Clock Tower

people who died defending them, and there are cannon marks still visible on the walls. Beside the last, the 15th-century **Loha Pol** (Iron Gate), are numerous *sati* handprints.

The palace, as it exists today, was only completed in 1853. It was divided in two, with the *zenana* (harem) to the left, and the men's and public apartments to the right. Inside, it is rich with treasures. Rooms are lush with sandalwood, *faux bois*, real marble and marble effect, lacy *jalis*, and painted panels and ceilings, reaching their most magnificent in the **Phool Mahal** (Flower Palace) with its gilded sandalwood ceiling that used 28kg of gold. Even better is the superb collection of furniture, which includes a richly inlaid stone table in the **Khabka Mahal**, several lavishly decorated royal cradles in the **Jhanki Mahal**, and a

fantastic set of palanquins and elephant *howdahs*. There are also collections of miniature paintings in the **Umaid Vilas**, musical instruments and costumes in the **Ajit Vilas,** and old manuscripts in the **Maharaja Mansingh Pushtak Prakash**. The arms collection includes the ornate swords of Timur and Akbar, and there are even campaign tents used by Maharaja Abhai Singh, and Mughal emperors Shah Jahan and Aurangzeb.

Beyond the main palace buildings are the stables and guardrooms, a wide rampart and gun emplacements. The cannons were looted from Gujarat after the defeat of Ahmadabad in 1730. From the ramparts, there are stupendous views of the city below. The prevalent blue traditionally marks the Brahmin houses, but its use has become more widespread because of the cooling and insect repellent properties of indigo mixed in the paint.

4km from the city centre, up a very steep hill. A lift is also available. Open: daily, 10am–5pm. Guided tours only within the palace. Admission & photo charge.

Sardar market

At the centre of the old town, at the foot of the cliff, is one of the best bazaars in Rajasthan, where acres of covered stalls surround a huge open-air market selling a vast array of fruit and vegetables, spices and cooking pots, textiles and trinkets. This is not a particularly good place for souvenir shopping, but the atmosphere is electric. The **English Clock Tower** was built by Maharaja Sardar Singh, and completed in 1915.

Best visited in the morning or late afternoon.

Umaid Bhavan

This stolid, 'Indo-Deco' palace, designed by British architect, H V Lanchester, for Maharaja Umaid Singh, was the last and largest ever built of Rajasthan's palaces. Conceived as a famine relief project, it was sited, on the advice of a holy man, on bedrock, with no water supply. Between 1929 and 1943, 3,000 builders and craftsmen were employed to build the 347-room palace, blasting foundation trenches from the rock – to construct a road and a railway (in order to transport the materials), and to bore for water.

Members of the royal family still live upstairs, and there is a small museum here, which contains a model and blueprints of the palace, model planes, and Jodhpuri history, art and crafts. The palace now also houses the city's most luxurious hotel.
Umaid Bhavan Rd. Tel: (0291) 2433316. Museum open: daily 9am–5pm. Admission charge for all but residential guests.

Umaid Gardens

At the centre of these green and shady gardens, laid out in 1909, with topiary elephants and camels, stands the **government museum**. It has some fine silver, enamel, porcelain, statuary and inlay work, but more interesting is the delightful toy collection, which includes ivory trains, cars and elephants, lively models of people at work, and crockery carved from rock salt. There is also the usual natural history section with displays of stuffed crocodiles and tigers in mortal combat, and ageing things in pickling jars. Nearby there is a small zoo with the usual monkeys and deer.
High Court Rd. Museum open: 10am–4.30pm. Closed: Fri. Admission charge.

JODHPUR ENVIRONS
Balsamand Summer Palace

First dammed in 1159 by Balak Rao Parihar, this delightful rainwater lake is a cool oasis amidst the rocky hills. The summer palace and gardens, heavy with mango trees, were laid out in 1936, and have now become a hotel complex.
9km northeast of Jodhpur. Open: daily 9am–6pm. Admission charge.

Mandore

Inhabited since the late Gupta period (5th–6th century AD), Mandnayapura, the original capital of Marwar, once had a 10-km long wall protecting a population of 50,000. It was captured by the Rathores in 1381, and effectively abandoned when the court was transferred to Jodhpur in 1459. The ruins now stand in shady gardens, and are entered via the **Ajit Pol**, the gate that was built as a celebration of Ajit Singh's victory over the Mughals in 1707.

Highlights of Mandore include: the graphic **Hall of Heroes**, a rock wall with high relief, brightly painted depictions of local heroes such as Pabuji and Chamunda (1707–49), and the crowded modern **Shrine of 30 Crore** (300 million) **Gods**, among them Brahma, Lakshmi and Kali. The **Pleasure Palace of Abhai Singh** now encloses a small museum. Mandore remained the royal cremation ground, and there are numerous memorial *chhatris* and temples, both Hindu and Jain, the earliest of which (on the hill) date from

the 8th century. The finest are the memorials of Maharajas Jaswant Singh (1638–78) and Ajit Singh (1678–1731), the second of whom was cremated along with six queens and 58 concubines.
10km north of Jodhpur. Open: daily sunrise–sunset. Museum section open: 10am–4.30pm. Closed: Fri.
Free admission.

Osiyan

Osiyan was a major trading centre on the camel caravan routes during the Gupta period (3rd–6th century AD). It is now a small market town surrounded by sand dunes. Twenty-three Jain and Hindu 5th- to 11th-century temples still stand in three separate clusters. The largest of the Jain temples (dating from the 8th to the 10th centuries) is dedicated to Mahavira, founder of Jainism, with an idol made of milk and sand, covered in 400g of gold, and said to be 2,500 years old.

The ancient Chamunda temple nearby (up 145 steps) houses a statue said to have appeared magically out of the rock. Both statue and temple are drowned in tinsel and tin foil.
58km north of Jodhpur.
Free admission.

Village safaris

See p147.

Lush gardens surround the ruins of Mandore, the old capital of Marwar

Mud huts and millet

The day begins at the household shrine, where every woman makes a quick offering to the gods. Women also fetch the water, cook the meals and look after the small children, then work with the men in the fields, growing millet and maize, chillies and vegetables. From about the age of five, the children join them, looking after chickens or cattle, and helping with the harvest. Cattle and water buffalo are crucial to rural life, providing muscle power for ploughing, turning the irrigation wheels and producing milk. On the rare occasions when there is meat with the basic menu of vegetables and *chapatis*, it will almost certainly be goat. Rajasthan does have large flocks of sheep, however, and in the desert, where melons and bitter cucumbers sprawl out across the sand for only a few short weeks, the camel is king (*see p146*). In their spare time, people weave, embroider or make pots. Some one-caste villages specialise as makers of toys or musical instruments, iron workers or saddlers.

Living close to the land and at the whim of the elements, nature is venerated and celebrated in a host of festivals marking the seasons, the harvests, and the human rites of passage (*see pp24–5*). Bright colours, whirling dances and noisy instruments bring a gaiety to life that is heightened during the local *mela*, a medieval-style market, livestock

market, fair and even religious festival, crucial to the survival of isolated communities.

Nearly three-quarters of India's population still lives a traditional life of subsistence farming. Most villagers are relatively poor. They live in simple

thatched huts, sleep on rope cots (*charpais*), or on the floor, fetch water from communal wells, and wash in a nearby stream or with water from shallow-dug hand pumps. Few have any education, and medical facilities are patchy in the extreme. Electricity lines may have reached many places, but power surges through erratically. Many in isolated pockets have just enough to eat, and live from day to day.

The cities may be vast and impossibly crowded, but over 650 million people still live in villages across India, their life simple and full of hard work. Although they may be very poor, their day-to-day existence is infinitely more pleasant than in the dirt and disease-ridden city slums.

Mount Abu

Mount Abu huddles among the rocks on a 1,220-m granite table mountain at the far southwestern end of the Aravalli Hills. It was here that the sage Vasishta conducted the sacred rituals by fire which created the four most powerful Rajput clans. From 1882 onwards, it became the head-quarters of the British Resident. There are hundreds of small temples in the vicinity, ranging from the ancient cave temple of Adhar Devi, to the most recent, a vast, pink *Shiva lingam* in the town centre.

Nakki Lake – popular with honeymooners

185km west of Udaipur and 326km southwest of Jodhpur, with good roads. The nearest rail station is Abu Rd, 30km south, with bus and jeeps connecting. Tourist Information Office: Opposite bus stand. Tel: (02974) 243151.

Adhar Devi Temple

This ancient temple is dedicated to the serpent goddess, Arbuda, patron of the town, who formed the mountain in order to save the sacred cow, Nandi, from drowning in an abyss. To reach the temple, climb the 360 steps, squeeze through a narrow cleft between two massive rocks, and enter the central cave temple on hands and knees, beneath a towering overhang. The black-painted marble idol, riding a solid gold tiger, is claimed to be about 5,000 years old.

2km north of town, off Subhash Rd. Open: sunrise–sunset. Free admission.

Art gallery and museum

A few interesting ceramics, glass plates, and bronzes lurk, totally unlabelled, beneath the dust of the official, poorly maintained, government museum.

Opposite Rajasthali, off Raj Bhavan Rd. Open: 10am–5pm. Closed Fri. Free admission.

Nakki Talav (Lake)

The holiday centre of Mount Abu, this sparkling blue artificial lake is said to have been gouged from the earth by the gods, using their fingernails (*nakh* means nail). There are boats for hire, gardens, photographers with fancy tinsel costumes for you to dress up in, and souvenirs by the ton. Nearby is the jazzed-up 14th-century **Raghunath Temple**. Several massive boulders crowning the surrounding hills have amusing names. Toad Rock is the most obvious, but look also for the Nun, the Camel and Nandi (bull).

On the western edge of the town centre. Nakki Lake Rd circles the entire lake. Rowing boats and pedaloes available for hire from the jetty by Gandhi Park. Free admission.

View points

Several points around the edge of the plateau offer spectacular views across the plains. The best are **Honeymoon Point** (Anadra Point) and **Sunset Point**, where hundreds of people gather to watch the sunset every evening in a carnival atmosphere of pony rides and souvenir sellers. **Bailey's Walk** is a pleasant 5km route from Nakki Lake to Sunset Point.

Honeymoon Point: 2.5km northwest on Ganesh Rd; Sunset Point: 2km southwest on Sunset Point Rd. Free admission.

Mount Abu

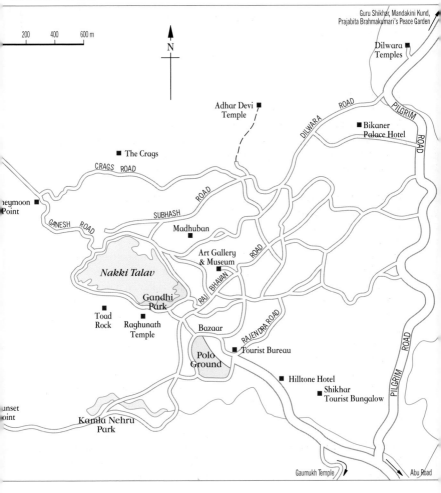

MOUNT ABU ENVIRONS
Dilwara temples

This complex of five marble Jain temples is one of the finest in Rajasthan, worth braving the queues and guards.

On the left, as you enter, is the relatively simple **Chaumukha Temple** (1458). Directly ahead is the earliest and most magnificent **Vimal Vasahi Temple**, built from 1031 by Vimal Shah, a Gujarati minister to King Bhim Devi I. He employed 1,500 artisans and 1,200 labourers for 14 years. Heralded by a column of white marble elephants, the cross-legged image of Adinath, the first *tirthankara*, sits under a dome intricately sculpted with scenes from the lives of the gods. The large courtyard has 52 cells and a superb colonnade of rampantly joyful pillars. Up the steps, the spectacular **Luna Vasahi Temple** was built in 1231 by two wealthy brothers, Vastupal and Tejpal, both also Gujarati ministers. Dedicated to Neminath, it is similar in style to the Vimal Vasahi Temple, but if anything, the delicacy of the sculpture is even more perfect, culminating in a massive, central, many-layered lotus, carved from a single block. The **Peetalhar Temple** (Rishabh Deoji), built by Brahma Shah in 1489, but not completed, has a huge brass (*peetal*) statue of Adinath. The temple of **Mahaveer Swami** was added in 1582.

3.5km northeast of town, on Pilgrim Rd. Open: daily noon–6pm for non-Jains. Free admission. Strictly no leather or photography (cameras not allowed inside).

ATTENTION PLEASE.
RULES FOR ENTRY IN TEMPLES
ENTRY : FREE.
VISITING HOURS 12ᴍᴍ TO 6ᴘᴍ (MORNING HOURS RESERVED FOR POOJA, WORSHIP FOR JAINS.
PERSONAL ARTICLES LIKE BAGS, SHOES, UMBRELLAS, FIRE-ARMS, EATABLES, DRINKABLES, ALL TYPES OF LEATHER – ARTICLES, RADIO TRANSISTOR, CAMERA ... NOT ALLOWED.
NONE SHALL ENTER THE TEMPLE WITH BETEL OR ANY KIND OF EATABLES IN THE MOUTH. KINDLY THROW-OUT & WASH THE MOUTH. SMOKING IS PROHIBITED.
DO NOT TOUCH PIECES OF ART & SCULPTURES WITH YOUR HAND, ANY PART – BODY OR ANY OTHER THING.
DO NOT ENTER ANY OF THE CELLS WHERE JAINS IDOLS, GODS & GODESSES ARE ENSHRINED.
SECURITY STAFF HAS RIGHT TO CHECK THE VANITY BAGS & BELONGINGS OF ANY BODY AT ENTRANCE OR ANY TIME WHILE IN TEMPLE.
IN TEMPLE CAMPUS, MOVING WITH HAND-IN-HAND, HAND ON SHOULDIER OR WAISTE IS STRICTLY PROHIBITED.
KINDLY OBSERVE ABOVE RULES & INSTRUCTIONS GIVEN BY THE TEMPLE PERSONNEL ON DUTY TO MAINTAIN & PRESERVE THE SANCTITY AND SACREDNESS OF THE TEMPLES.
— CHIEF WARDEN.

Gaumukh Temple

Dedicated to Rama, this small temple (called the Cow's Mouth) is centred on a spring gushing from the mouth of a marble cow. In the Hindu creation myth, the world is formed by a cow licking salt; the source of the Ganges has the same name, that is, Gaumukh. This is said to be the site of the ancient fire rituals which created the four great Rajput clans. *4km south of Mount Abu. Free admission. Entrance down 700 very steep steps.*

Guru Shikhar

At 1,722m, this is the highest peak between the Himalayas and the southern Nilgiri Hills. On the summit are a radar station and a temple, the latter dedicated to Guru Dattatreya (an incarnation of Vishnu), and reached by 367 steps. *16km north of Mount Abu. Free admission (except to the radar station).*

Mandakini Kund

Sitting on a site held sacred for 5,000 years, the Achaleshwar Temple has a small hole plummeting deep into the earth in place of the usual *lingam*. It was created by Shiva, who stamped hard to quieten the earthquakes plaguing the area, and no one has ever managed to measure its true depth. To the side of the hole is a small, rounded rock, said to be the toe of Lord Shiva.

Mandakini Kund, a stepped tank, was the water supply for the fort of **Achalgarh**, built on a nearby hill by the 15th-century Mewari ruler, Rana Kumbha. Beside the tank are lifesize statues of three buffaloes and the Parmar king Adipal. According to legend, in ancient times it was filled with *ghee* (melted butter). Each night, three demon buffaloes would sneak down and drink it dry. Eventually the sages took the problem to King Adipal, who cornered the demons and shot all three with one arrow.

11km north of Mount Abu on the road to Guru Shikhar. Free admission.

Prajabita Brahmakumari's Peace Garden

In 1984 the Brahma Kumari religious sect created this garden of flags and poinsettias to promote peace and harmony. The sect's Mount Abu headquarters includes a spiritual museum and university.

8km north of Mount Abu, on the road to Guru Shikhar. Open: daily 10am–noon & 2.30–5pm. Free admission.

The magnificent Dilwara temples are an all-year-round place of Jain pilgrimage

Ranthambhore

Ranthambhore, fed by several perennial rivers that have been dammed to form lakes, is a lush, green refuge in a largely semi-arid region. It is also one of the most popular game parks in the country. Wildlife sightings are almost certain along designated routes. The park is worth a visit for its landscape alone: delicate man-made pavilions nestle alongside emerald lakes in the cradle of verdant slopes of rolling hills, and on one side, the crumbling fort still towers protectively over its domain.

Sambar wallow in Ranthambhore Lake, a coveted prey of tigers. Nevertheless, their numbers are rising rapidly

The Fort

Built in AD 944 by a Chauhan ruler, Ranthambhore stands at the gateway between the Mughal north and central India. As a result, it became a political football, with control swinging backwards and forwards between Delhi and the Rajputs. Only one great tragedy is recorded by legend. In 1301, as Alauddin Khalji laid siege, Prince Hammir and his warriors went out to fight, telling the ladies of the court to commit *jauhar* should they lose sight of the standard. The Rajputs won, chasing the Sultan's troops into the distance. As the standard vanished, the ladies committed *jauhar* and Hammir's triumphant return was greeted by the sight of their bodies. He was so appalled that he too committed suicide. In 1569, the fort was eventually captured by Akbar, who handed it to the maharaja of Amber (Jaipur), ending its history as an independent kingdom.

The seven gates and massive curtain walls crowning a flat-topped, 225-m high hill with sheer sides and dramatic views, are still intact and forbidding. Near the entrance is Hammir's badly damaged but romantic palace (12th- to 13th-century), with mirrored rooms, fountains, and balconies overlooking the plain. There are also several water tanks and temples, of which the most important is an undistinguished 10th-century temple to Ganesh, now a popular place of pilgrimage. Those who visit leave the god reminders of their prayers; their old rags if they have asked for new clothes, and a little heap of stones representing a new house. He even gets thousands of wedding invitations a year!

National Park

Used as a hunting ground by the Maharaja of Jaipur, Ranthambhore became a game sanctuary in 1955, and one of the original nine Project Tiger reserves in 1972 (*see pp126–7*). The core area of about 400sq km became a National Park in 1980, and in 1992, the bordering Keladevi and Man Singh sanctuaries were added, with wildlife 'corridors' running between the protected areas. Of the total protected area only a very small portion remains open to the public.

Ranthambhore is said to be the one sanctuary in India where, especially between November and April, tiger sightings are almost certain – all it requires is patience and luck. Officially, there are about 30 tigers in the national park, and another six to nine in Keladevi. They are extremely solitary creatures, covering a wide territory, and are so well camouflaged that they fade into the thick undergrowth literally yards from the road.

Tigers or not, Ranthambhore has magic. Cavernous banyan trees drip roots, while the skinny twisted *dhok* trees scramble across the hills, turning flaming red in autumn. If tigers are rare, numerous other species are very visible. You will certainly see the antelopes – nilgai, sambar and cheetal – and the lucky ones may also find sloth bears, wild boar, chinkara, caracal, porcupines

and jackals. The lakes are filled with lotus and crocodiles, and 264 species of bird have been recorded. And if that were not enough, the whole area is littered with ruined pavilions and *chhatris*, the finest of which is the **Jogi Mahal**, the old guesthouse by the lake, now, unfortunately, closed to visitors.

Ranthambhore is 14km from Sawai Madhopur, the nearest town and station; 157km southeast from Jaipur; and 361km south from Delhi. Tourist information, and tours by jeep or lorry bookable at the Project Tiger Office, Sawai Madhopur. Tel: (07462) 223402. Open: 10am–5pm. Fort: entrance beside the park gate: Free admission sunrise–sunset. National Park open: daily 6–9am & 3–6pm. Closed: 1 Jul–30 Sep. Only guided tours in Project Office vehicles are allowed, strictly on allocated routes. Fees for entrance, vehicle hire, guide and cameras. Also visit the **Dastkar Kendra** *(crafts centre) opposite Kutalpura village beyond the park along the same road. Tel: (07462) 252052.*

Ranthambhore's jungle-clad hills are one of the last havens of the tiger

Project Tiger

By 1973 the world population of tigers was down to around 3,600, about 1,800 of them in India. Project Tiger was born out of a last-ditch effort to save them from extinction. There are now 28 nature reserves within the scheme, two of them, Ranthambhore and Sariska, in Rajasthan. Planned eco-development efforts helped people move out of the park areas, which were then fenced off. Each park is now surrounded by a buffer zone, where villagers can graze cattle and collect wood, but not live or farm. Locals are compensated for the loss of land and any stock or crops destroyed by wild animals. They are also being helped to find alternative sources of income. The Ranthambhore Foundation is an especially active group, creating eco-awareness, medical, economic, and educational opportunities.

Although Project Tiger initially succeeded in raising India's total count of tigers by a substantial degree (about 4,000), its very success has brought back the poachers, and tigers are once more fighting for survival against habitat destruction and the rapacious Chinese alternative medicine market. Indian tigers currently total about 2,400. Game wardens talk nervously about parks being for all species, not just tigers. They seem to be preparing the world for the day when, very soon, they are obliged to admit that the tiger is extinct in the wild.

The tiger is India's national animal. Project Tiger aims to protect these magnificent creatures from extinction by loss of habitat and by human predators

TIGER TIGER BURNING BRIGHT

Largest of the great cats, weighing up to 200kg, the tiger is remarkably versatile, surviving in a variety of habitats and climates, and able to swim and climb trees. They do need space, however; a single male will have a territory of up to 100sq km, which he will share with three to five females, each of whom may have three to six cubs. The cubs stay with the mother until about the age of two and a half. Tigers stalk, rather than chase, grabbing the prey from behind and killing it swiftly. Ideally, they look for a large animal which will last them four or five days. Once adult, their only predators are human, many of whom still sadly believe that the skins look better on a wall, and that eating powdered bones will increase their courage and sexual prowess.

Udaipur

Udaipur's present maharana is the 76th in an unbroken line of rulers, making it the oldest surviving dynasty in the world. Its founder, Udai Singh II, escaped death as a baby by a pretender to the throne, who had already assassinated his brother, the ruler of Mewar, in 1536. Word reached the nursery just in time, and the young prince's nurse, Panna Bai, switched the baby with her own. A few minutes later she watched helplessly as her own baby was disembowelled by the traitor.

Miniature paintings are sold in homes and shops

Udaipur

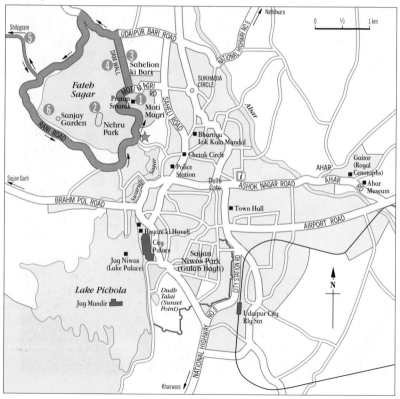

The grieving mother then smuggled Udai Singh out of Chittorgarh to Kumbhalgarh, where he grew up under the protection of the governor – the same man who would eventually help him regain his throne when he was 15. In 1557, Udai Singh came across a holy man who told him to establish a new city on the very spot where they had met, prophesying, correctly, that it would never be defeated in battle.

Within two years graceful Udaipur was born, on the shores of Lake Pichola. The city had a 10-km long wall and 11 gates. Mewar was the only Rajput state that proudly withstood Mughal domination. Even today, it is relatively untouched by outside influences. With a population of some 350,000, Udaipur is a peaceful place, with white buildings mirrored in expanses of blue water. *374km southwest from Jaipur; good road, rail, and air connections. Tourist Information Office: Fateh Memorial, Suraj Pol. Tel: (0294) 411535.*

Note: Map numbers refer to Fateh Sagar Tour *on pages 138–9.*

Pratap Singh

Son of Udai Singh, the founder of Udaipur, Pratap Singh is one of the greatest heroes of Rajasthan. Succeeding his father in 1572, at the height of the conflict with Akbar, he swore never to submit to the Mughal emperor, or to sleep in his own bed until Mewar was safe. Taking to the hills with a band of followers, he waged war for 25 years. Legend says his favourite horse, Chetak, jumped over a wide chasm with a broken leg, in order to save his master from Akbar's forces at the battle of Haldighati (*see p140*). At Pratap Singh's death in 1597, Mewar was still a free state.

Monumental arches lead to the bathing *ghats*

City Palace

The largest palace complex in Rajasthan is in fact a series of several palaces, large and small, tacked on by successive maharanas (as they were known here) over 400 years, with such success that they run together seamlessly. About half of the complex (to the right) is still the private residence of the royal family. Part of the palace is now a museum, and part includes two hotels, the very grand **Shiv Niwas**, where you can stop for a refreshing drink, and the less opulent **Fateh Prakash Palace**. The lavish central portion is open to the public.

Built in 1725, the triple-arched **Tripolia Pol** leads through to the massive **Bada Chowk** (outer courtyard), large enough to house the massed army of Mewar, including 100 elephants. It used to be the custom for the maharana to be weighed under the arches, and his weight in gold distributed to the poor. Near the entrance to the **government museum**, with its memorabilia of Rana Pratap Singh (Udai Singh's son, and a legendary hero who defeated even the great Mughal, Akbar, *see p129*), is a family tree, dating back to 566. For the last 200 years, all the maharanas have been adopted (from within the Sisodia family), as a curse gave them only daughters. The last maharana eventually had two sons, but ironically, only after he had lost his title.

The interior of the palace winds through a long series of rooms, some very plain, others enormously decorative, with workmanship and taste ranging from the sublime to the ridiculous. The 300-year-old **Bada Mahal** appears to have a terraced garden

Technicolour glass in the City Palace, Udaipur

and bathing pool on the fourth floor; in fact, it is a hill which was cut away as the palace was built around it. The **Dilkhush Mahal** (Jovial Palace) has a series of magnificent miniature frescoes, and was probably used for European guests. Even better are those in the entrancingly decorated **Krishna Mahal**, now a memorial to a 16-year-old princess who, in the 19th century, committed suicide rather than risk war between the clans of two rival suitors.

Beyond this is the oriental **Manek Mahal** (Ruby Palace), in which the 18th-century **Chini Chitrashala** is decorated in blue and white Chinese and Dutch tiles, swapped for opium (once a major local industry). The upper storeys formed the *zenana* (*see p19*), and now house the museum collection, which includes silver and gold ornaments, and miniature paintings. Several rooms are elaborately decorated with paintings, coloured glass and tiles, and culminate in the gaudy Queen's Make-up Room, which boasts a two-way mirror that allowed the maharana to watch the queen unobserved.

Downstairs, the **Mor Chowk** (Peacock Courtyard) takes its name from three mosaic peacocks. Off the courtyard are the public apartments with an almost psychedelic dining room, lined with glass tiles surrounding a huge 19th-century representation of the Sun God. *Lake Pichola. Tel: (0294) 528016. Open: daily 9.30am–4.30pm. Admission &*

photo charge. Separate fee for the palace museum and government museum.

Bagore ki Haveli

This 18th-century house on the banks of Lake Pichola was built by a minor raja. It served as a royal guest house for a number of years, and has a small museum. The archway next door leads down to the **Gangaur Ghat**, where men and women gather in separate sections to bathe and do their laundry. The *ghats* are lined with numerous small shrines. *Lake Pichola. Tel: (0294) 523858. Open: daily 10am–5pm. Closed: Sun. Admission charge. Free admission to the bathing* ghats *(strictly no photographs).*

The extensive City Palace complex, built over 400 years by successive maharanas

Ahar

The small, insignificant archaeological site of Dhum Kot produced a fascinating record of life in the area as far back as 4,000 BC, but like many secondary places on the tourist map, it is somewhat underwhelming to look at. Beside it is a small archaeological museum with numerous pre-Aryan exhibits, including some stunning Copper Age pots and later temple statuary. The cenotaphs of 19 Mewar rulers are clustered nearby.
Ahar Rd, 4km from Lake Pichola (no tel). Open: 10am–4.30pm. Closed: Fri. Admission charge.

Bhartiya Lok Kala Mandal (Folklore Museum)

This is a delightful if sadly neglected folk museum, stuffed full of entertaining treasures. It is very much a working museum with craft workshops, an academic wing collecting recordings of folk tales and music, in addition to its own highly acclaimed dance and puppet troops. Among the exhibits are displays on turban tying, decorative henna patterns on hands, village shrines, *phads*, *pichhwais* and *kavads* (*see pp134–5*), and puppets. The curator is happy to talk for hours about the local crafts and traditions of the region.
Chetak Circle. Tel: (0294) 529296. Open: daily 9am–6pm, performances 6–7pm. Admission & photo charge.

Cenotaphs

The memorial *chhatris* of the royal family are clustered in an overgrown garden. The oldest tombs, furthest from

Lake Pichola is the tranquil setting for a fairytale palace

the gate, were built of lime-covered brick, while later additions were of marble. The two massive temple-like structures belong to Maharanas Amar Singh (r.1597–1620) and Sangram Singh (r.1710–34), both of whom were noted for their bravery against the Mughals.
Ahar Rd, 4km from Lake Pichola.
The gates are locked, but the doorkeeper will gladly admit you at any time.
Free admission (baksheesh *expected*).

Dudh Talai Park

At the top of this small hillside park, Sunset Point, with its cafés, street vendors and children's playground, provides the city's best view of the sunset over Lake Pichola.

Jagdish Temple

Approached by steep steps guarded by stone elephants and carved all over with jolly dancing girls, this temple was built by Maharana Jagat Singh I in 1651. Inside are a massive black stone idol of Vishnu shown as Jagannath, Lord of the Universe, and a bronze statue of Garuda, half man, half eagle, vehicle of Vishnu.
North of the City Palace. Free admission.

Lake Fateh Sagar

See pp138–9.

Lake Pichola

First built in the 14th century, Lake Pichola was strengthened and enlarged by Maharana Udai Singh while he was building the city in the 16th century, and now covers about 8sq km. It is fed only by rainwater and drainage from the hills around, and in times of severe drought has dried up completely.

Jag Mandir

Built on a yellow sandstone base and surrounded by carved elephants, this small island palace, south of Jag Niwas, was founded in 1615 by Maharana Karan Singh as a royal guesthouse, and takes its name from Jagat Singh I, who completed the work. In 1623, the Mughal prince Khurram (later to take the throne as Shah Jahan) who had rebelled against his father, took refuge here.

Jag Niwas (Lake Palace)

Built as a summer palace on an island in Lake Pichola in 1746 by Maharana Jagat Singh II, this is a romantic fairytale confection of delicate white marble skimming the surface of the lake. It shot to fame, courtesy of James Bond, as the island home of *Octopussy*, and has become one of the classic images of Rajasthan. Since 1962 it has been the luxurious Lake Palace Hotel, replete with antique furniture, trellised balconies and wall frescoes.
Boat tours round the lake and to the Jag Mandir leave from the Lake Palace jetty beside the City Palace. Tel: (0294) 527961.
Open: Apr–Sept 8–11am, 3–6pm; Oct–Mar 10–noon, 2–5pm. Only guests or diners are allowed inside the Lake Palace. Boat ticket includes the meal ticket.

Sahelion ki Bari and Shilpgram

See p139.

Sajjan Niwas Park

This lush park, with a splendid rose garden (the **Gulab Bagh**), laid out by Maharana Sajjan Singh (r.1874–84), has a small zoo and a 2-km toy train track.
Lake Palace Rd. Open: daily 10am–5pm.

Surviving Hindu paintings stretch back to at least the 14th century. The earliest examples were painted on banana and palm leaf, but beside them lay a host of other media including frescoes, cloth paintings known as *pichhwais* (hung in temples) or *phads* (used in telling folk tales), and little wooden travelling *kavads* (box theatres/temples painted like strip cartoons). Most concentrated on religious themes and were designed to tell a story inspired by epic tales, such as the *Ramayana,* and *Gita Govinda* (which celebrates the divine love of Radha and Krishna), and by the *ragas* (musical mood poems). These paintings were brightly coloured, rich with natural life and, in many cases, a natural eroticism. With the coming of Islam, which disapproved of human representation in art, the illustration of manuscripts developed. Painting in the more formal, softly coloured Persian style was introduced to India by Emperor

Humayun, who brought back two artists on his return from exile in Persia in 1556. With a religion that disapproved of iconography, the Mughal painters were strictly secular. Geometric patterns

with the Rajput princes, taking their Persian-influenced Mughal style back into Hindu art. The brushes of individual artists helped to shape distinctive regional schools of painting that still exist today, from the elegant minutiae of courtly Udaipur, to the sketchier, bolder freedom of Jodhpur. Today, tiny, delicate miniature paintings of traditional themes are reproduced on paper and silk in exact copies of their splendid 300-year-old originals.

Modern artists still use the same techniques followed by Persian, Mughal and Rajput miniature painters of old

were accompanied by flora and fauna, and riotous scenes of feasts and hunts, tender love stories and stately processions. Akbar, though illiterate, was ever curious throughout his life, and began to hire Indian artists to illustrate Hindu texts for him to study. Inevitably, the two styles began to merge.

Ironically, it was the puritanical Aurangzeb who prompted the final stage of evolution. He disapproved of frivolity and was determined to stamp out what he saw as idolatry. The painters fled his court to outlying provinces, many of them seeking shelter

Rambling hilltop Kumbhalgarh was the last refuge of countless Mewar kings

UDAIPUR ENVIRONS
Ambika Mata Temple
This ancient and venerated temple is a popular place of pilgrimage. Built in AD 960 and dedicated to the fierce goddess Durga, it has particularly fine and sensual carvings of celestial nymphs and beautiful women.

Jagat, 50km southeast of Udaipur. Free admission.

Jaisamand
See p142.

Kumbhalgarh
The second most important fort in Mewar, this magnificent mountain ruin sprawls massively across the hills on a plateau over 1,000m high. It was built in 1458 by Rana Kumbha, who was also responsible for some of the finest buildings at Chittorgarh (*see pp82–3*), and became a refuge for the royal family. Udai Singh was brought up and

crowned here after his escape from assassination (*see p128*). It was sacked only once, by the combined armies of the Mughals, Amber and Marwar, when its water was poisoned.

A 36-km long outer wall encloses an inner fort area of over 12sq km, with a steep approach through seven massive gateways. The fort had everything needed to withstand a lengthy siege, including fields, water, kitchen gardens and 365 temples. A village still thrives in the outer courtyard. The main palace building, the **Badal Mahal** (Cloud Palace), occupies the summit, approached by a steep, winding footpath. Several rooms have fine wall paintings, but the real stars are the superb panoramic views and the sheer drama of the setting.

A 578sq km **wildlife sanctuary** in the surrounding hills is home to leopards, chinkara, sloth bear, porcupines and flying squirrels, and is the only successful breeding ground of wolves in India. The neighbouring village, **Ghanerao**, has fine painted *havelis*, marble *chhatris*, and a medieval castle and hunting lodge, now open to guests. Camel, horse and goat treks are on offer in the surrounding jungle.

63km north of Udaipur. Open: sunrise– sunset. Free admission. The palace keys are held by a guide (baksheesh expected).

Ranakpur
Set in a peaceful, wooded river valley, approachable through the Kumbhalgarh sanctuary, this complex of Jain temples is the largest and one of the most holy in Rajasthan. It is hugely popular with

pilgrims, and has three dormitory hostels and a massive dining room to prove it. From the tourist's point of view, it also includes some of the most beautiful temple carvings in the whole of India.

The complex was founded in the mid-14th century, but most of the buildings date from the 15th. The smaller, outlying temples are relatively simple. The highlight is the **Chaumukha Temple**, a huge walled complex covering 3,600sq m, on a high stone plinth, approached by steep steps. Inside are a staggering 29 halls and 1,444 pillars. Carved from a creamy white marble, made translucent by the sunshine, each pillar is different, finer and more intricate than the last. An extraordinary imagination has created images of goddesses and nymphs, dancers and elephants, scenes of daily life and

glorious fantasy that soar far beyond the mundane. Access to the roof leads to a whole new world of elaborate domes, spires and prayer flags. At the centre is a huge, four-faced idol of the first *tirthankara*, Adinath, Giver of Truth. *95km north of Udaipur on the Jodhpur Rd. Open: to non-Jains, noon–5pm. Free admission, but photo charge. Strictly no leather or photos of the idols (also read the amazingly detailed list of prohibitions by the main office).*

Sajjan Garh (Monsoon Palace)

Built by Maharana Sajjan Singh in the late-18th century, this little palace is perched high on a steep hill overlooking Lake Pichola. The views of the city are superb, but the palace itself is closed. *About 15km from the city, up very steep, poorly maintained hairpin bends. Allow about three hours for the round trip.*

Intricate and varied carving on each of the pillars at Ranakpur temple

Tour: Around Fateh Sagar

This tour covers the entire 9km circumference of green and tranquil Fateh Sagar which is bordered by hills. A good alternative is to walk the east shore. For the main route, see the Udaipur town plan on page 128.

Allow three hours.

The international boundaries on this r are neither purported to be correct nc authenticated by Survey of India direc

Start beside the bridge linking the Fateh Sagar and smaller Swarup Sagar. Follow the lakeshore road north to the entrance of Moti Magri Park.

1 Pratap Smarak

Moti Magri (Pearl Hill) was the site of the first city of Udaipur, although only a few fragmentary walls mark the spot. The steep hill is now a park. At the top, the Pratap Smarak is a monument to Maharana Pratap Singh, the only Rajput ruler never to submit to the Mughals. A splendid equestrian bronze shows the gallant maharana riding his favourite horse, Chetak (*see p129*). There are also a bird garden and small museum.

Turn right out of the entrance, and follow the road past the souvenir stands to the boat area and jetty. From here ferries run regularly to Nehru Park. There are also pedaloes and rowing boats for hire.

2 Nehru Park

Work on this attractive island began in 1937 under the auspices of Maharana Bhupal Singh who intended to build a water palace as a famine relief project. The palace was never completed, and after Independence the island was turned into a public garden, named after prime minister Jawaharlal Nehru.

Maharana Pratap and his valiant steed, Chetak, who died in the battle of Haldighati

Rajasthan has a strong craft heritage

Continue round the lake. A road to the right, round the back of Moti Magri, leads to the Sahelion ki Bari.

3 Sahelion ki Bari (Garden of the Maids of Honour)

Built by Maharana Sangram Singh (r.1710–34) for his ten daughters, this must have been one of the most beautiful water gardens in Rajasthan. It is filled with delights such as the Rain without Cloud Fountain (listen to the sound when the water is turned on), and the elaborate lily-filled Shakuntala Fountain, named after the eldest daughter. Jets of water shooting from the elephants' trunks were designed to create rainbows. A small children's museum exhibits curiosities such as a pickled scorpion and a bust of the Greek mathematician Archimedes.

Return to the lakeshore road and cross the dam wall.

4 Dam wall

Fateh Sagar was originally constructed in 1678, but its dam was washed away by heavy floods. The elegant dam wall with its string of small pavilions was rebuilt in 1889 by Maharana Fateh Singh, after whom the lake is now named.

The road turns back along the western shore. Towards the end, a well-signed turning to the right leads to the Shilpgram.

5 Shilpgram

Founded in 1989, this delightful arts and crafts complex has a small, beautifully designed museum with costumes, headgear and shoes, kitchen utensils, musical instruments, toys and ornaments, and a complex of authentic village dwellings from Rajasthan, Gujarat, Goa and Maharashtra, built by local people out of traditional materials. Musicians, dancers, puppeteers and acrobats regularly perform in the outdoor arena.

Return to the lakeshore road and follow it back to your starting point. Halfway along the south shore is Sanjay Garden.

6 Sanjay Garden

Another tiny island garden, with a splendid multi-coloured fountain, this was named after Indira Gandhi's younger son, Sanjay, who was killed in a flying accident in New Delhi.

Pratap Smarak Moti Magri Hill.
Sahelion ki Bari Moti Magri Rd.
Open: daily 9am–6pm. Admission charge.
Shilpgram Fateh Sagar Rani Rd.
There are crafts demonstrations and sales at weekends; also a swimming pool and camel rides.
Open: daily (in season) 10am–6pm.
Admission charge.

The international boundaries on this m
are neither purported to be correct no
authenticated by Survey of India direct

Tour: North from Udaipur

This drive through the Aravalli Hills offers a delightful
glimpse of rural Rajasthan, and visits two magnificent
sites, Kumbhalgarh and Ranakpur (*see pp136–7*), along
with smaller but significant temples and historic places.
Allow one very long day; preferably two.

*Leave Udaipur on NH8, heading
northeast aross the hills to Kailashpur.*

1 Nagda and Eklingji Temples
This famous complex of 108 temples

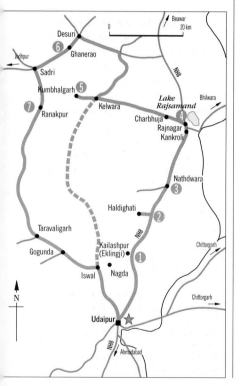

in **Kailashpur** village was first built in
AD 734, and then rebuilt in the 15th
century after it had been destroyed by
Aurangzeb. Dedicated to Eklingji (a
manifestation of Shiva), the Mewar
family deity, the main temple includes
an ornate, pyramid-roofed, pillared
hall, and a four-faced black marble
image of Shiva. At nearby Nagda, the
ancient Mewar capital, a 15th-century
Adbhutji Jain temple and two 11th-
century Vishnu temples standing near
a small lake display some intricate
carving.
*Continue north through a rocky gorge
along NH8. After about 12km, a turning
to the left leads 5km to the Haldighati
battlefield.*

2 Haldighati
This is the site of Pratap Singh's most
famous battle, on 21 June 1576. The
maharana came face to face with Man
Singh of Jaipur, leader of the Mughal
army, mounted on an elephant. Pratap's
pure white horse, Chetak, leapt up to
strike the elephant which fled after
badly wounding Chetak and Pratap
Singh. The valiant horse leapt a stream
to carry his master to safety before
dying, and is revered as a true hero of

Mewar, with a monument built in his honour (see p138).

Return to the main road and continue northwards for another 8km to Nathdwara. Turn left past the bus station, park and walk through the bazaar to the temple.

3 Nathdwara Temple

In 1669, followers of the Vallabhachari sect (Krishna devotees) fled from Mathura and Aurangzeb's tyranny with a sacred black idol of Lord Krishna. At Nathdwara, the wheels of their chariot sank, and taking it as a sign, they stopped and built a temple to house the image. Today, the temple is popular among Hindu pilgrims. Eight times daily a new *pichhwai* (painted handspun cloth telling the life of Krishna) is hung behind the statue. It is difficult for non-Hindus to get inside, but the buzzing bazaar is well worth a stop. Artists sell and display the 400-year-old craft, some of the paintings worth a handsome sum of money.

Return to the main road and continue north, following signs for Ajmer. Just beyond Kankroli, home of the Vaishnava Dwarikadheesh Temple, is Lake Rajsamand.

4 Lake Rajsamand

Lined by marble pavilions and *chhatris*, this pleasant lake was built in 1660 by Maharana Raj Singh following a severe drought. His wife Charumati built the Nauchowki Pavilion to honour her husband, who married her to save her from Aurangzeb. Other fine buildings include a palace and garden built by the 19th-century maharana, Sajjan Singh.

The road now runs through massive marble works to Khomsi, where you turn left for Charbhuja, which has another popular Vaishnava pilgrimage temple, and Kelwara. From here, it is 9km up a steep mountain road to Kumbhalgarh. There is also a road back to Udaipur.

5 Kumbhalgarh

See p136.

Go back down the hill to Kelwara and turn left for Ranakpur, 20km further on through Desuri and Sadri.

6 Ghanerao

Founded in 1606 by a Rathore ruler, this small village lies in a pass between the Jodhpur and Udaipur region. For such a small place, it has a remarkable variety of handsome red sandstone *havelis*, temples, stepwells and marble *chhatris*, and a gem of a castle. The present head of the ruling family organises treks to Kumbhalgarh and Ranakpur. Close by is the beautifully carved home of the erstwhile Jain prime minister Dayal Shah.

7 Ranakpur Jain temples

See pp136–7.

It is 95km back to Udaipur, via Gogunda and Iswal.

Eklingji Temple Kailashpur, 22km from Udaipur. Open: daily 5–7am, 10am–1pm & 5–7pm. Inner sanctum closed to non-Hindus.
Nagda Temples Free admission during daylight hours.
Nathdwara Temple Open: noon–1pm for non-Hindus (theoretically).

Getting away from it all

When forts and palaces, temples and museums have saturated the senses, the countryside around the major cities and historic sites is there to offer a haven of natural beauty and peace. In stark contrast to the pockets of forest and scrubland where natural life abounds, is the desert, where the stars dazzle you with their brilliance at night.

Wary deer – the primary prey of the tiger

NATIONAL PARKS
Desert National Park

In 1972, a massive 3,162sq km of the Thar Desert was designated a national park, ironically in order to preserve it from irrigation schemes (*see p6*) that would take away its geographical identity. Close to 30 villages are located within the park area in the relatively more habitable areas.

Several areas such as the Sam Dunes and Akal Fossil Park are now open to tourists, but the 300sq km core is dedicated to scientific study, and special permits are required to gain access to it. Animal life within the park includes chinkara, desert fox, desert cat and hare. This is also a breeding ground for the rare great Indian bustard, and a winter retreat for birds, including imperial sand grouse, demoiselle cranes, lesser bustard, and numerous raptors, including eagles, falcons and harriers.

60km southeast from Jaisalmer (285km west from Jodhpur). Enquire at Rajasthan Tourism Office about permits (see p105).

Jaisamand

This large and astonishingly beautiful lake, which extends over 160sq km and is ringed by gentle hills, was dammed by Maharana Jai Singh in 1685. Two royal summer palaces, the **Hawa Mahal** and the **Roothi Rani ka Mahal**, overlook the lake, while the dam wall is topped by marble *chhatris*, decorated with finely carved elephants, and a small but evocative Shiva temple.

Near the lake, a 52sq km wildlife sanctuary is the home of a wide variety of birds, as well as cheetal, chinkara, wild boar and leopard. The surrounding area is the Bheel tribal homeland.

48km southeast of Udaipur.
Free admission.

Keoladeo Ghana Bird Sanctuary

One of the world's great sanctuaries, this 29sq km birdland of marsh and savannah attracts a staggering 375 species of bird. It is a magnet for bird watchers, but also a haven of peace in which to escape urban India. Among the common bulbuls, doves, egrets and ducks are several species of birds of prey, heron, stork and owl, and a migrant population of rare Siberian cranes. Land animals include cheetal, sambar, *nilgai* (blue bull), blackbuck, jungle cats and pythons.

Qualified naturalists are available as tour

guides (ask at the gate), and most rickshaw-wallahs are also knowledgeable. No motorised transport inside; either walk, hire a bicycle, or use a cycle rickshaw (standard hourly rate). In season, rowing boats are available for marsh tours. Breeding season is Aug–Oct; the migrants arrive Oct–late Feb. Best viewing times are early morning and late afternoon. (See also p74.)

Kumbhalgarh Sanctuary
See p136.

Ranthambhore
See pp124–5.

Sariska
Once a royal hunting ground, Sariska has been, since 1979, a Project Tiger reserve (*see pp126–7*), consisting of a 480sq km national park, surrounded by an 800sq km wildlife sanctuary. Set in the rocky Aravalli Hills, it is a lovely wilderness of tangled woodlands and steep hills, interspersed by open savannah, lakes and waterholes. Within the sanctuary is the **Kankwari Fort** where Emperor Aurangzeb imprisoned his brother, Dara Shukoh, the rightful heir to the throne.

There are also some fascinating temples at **Bhartihari** (6km) and **Neelkanth** (3km). Apart from tigers, the animal population is large, with hyenas, leopards and jungle cats, foxes, jackals, wildboar, and plentiful sambar, cheetal and *nilgai*. There is also a thriving bird population. Unfortunately, access has now been restricted to one drive, and the undergrowth is so dense that it can be extremely difficult to spot anything more than a few yards from the road.

37km southwest of Alwar on the Jaipur road. Tourist Information Office: Project Tiger, Sariska Sanctuary. Tel: (0144) 2241333. Open: daily Oct–Mar 7am–4pm. Apr–Sept 6am–4.30pm. Project Tiger jeeps only allowed in core area. You will be accompanied by a guide, and must stick to the route. Admission charges per person, vehicle, and camera, plus jeep hire.

> **Minor Parks and Sanctuaries**
> **Darrah Game Sanctuary** 50km south of Kota. *See p90.*
> **Dhawa (Doli) Sanctuary** 45km southeast of Jodhpur.
> **Gajner Sanctuary** 35km west of Bikaner. *See p81.*
> **Sitamata Sanctuary** 200km east of Udaipur.
> **Tal Chapper Sanctuary** 200km northwest of Jaipur.

The blackbuck antelope lives on the plains of India but is under threat from humans

Often overshadowed by the cities, the architecture, and the sheer press of people, India has also a rich and varied natural world. Even in the cities, regiments of spiky Ashok (*Saraca indica*) trees line formal gardens; the *peepal* (*Ficus religiosa*), sacred since it shaded Buddha during his Enlightenment, is still used for shade and as medicine; and the glossy, rounded mango (*Mangifera indica*) tree, staple of royal orchards, is generous with hundreds of fruit. The ubiquitous *neem* (*Azadirachta indica*) is now internationally famous for its medicinal properties. Out of town, the twisted hardwood *dhok* (*Butea monosperma*), whose leaves flame in autumn, carpets the Aravalli Hills, while the thorny *kikar* (*Acacia arabica*) and

khejri (*Prosopis cinera*) dominate the desert.

For a few short weeks after the rains each year, the dunes glow with a million luminous yellow tennis balls, a melon-type creeping fruit known as the camel fruit or desert apple. Finest of all is the superb, pendulous banyan (*Ficus bengalensis*), with roots flowing earthwards from its massive branches.

Facing page above: the Sarus crane is now a rare sight in northern India
Facing page below: a monitor lizard emerges from a tree-hole
Above: the silver langur can be found in national parks and towns across Rajasthan

In the national parks, cheetal, with chestnut coats liberally spotted in white and branched antlers, daintily browse in the dappled woodland. The larger nilgai (blue bull), with a blue-grey sheen on its heavy body, splashes through the marshland, and in an open, grassy clearing is a herd of buff brown sambar, the male's antlers resplendent as the *Monarch of the Glen*. Far away, on the fringes of the desert, graze India's gazelles, the chinkara and the blackbuck.

A family of bush pigs rootles in a forest clearing, a shaggy sloth bear ambles through the forest, porcupines rustle their quills as they edge through the undergrowth, and a crocodile sunbathes on a sandbank. High up on the rocky crest, a spotted leopard sprawls along a branch eyeing up the local troop of langur monkeys. Its smaller relatives, the wild cats, prowl the grass like household mogs on a spree. Jackals and hyenas circle restlessly looking for the leftovers of someone else's meal. A python slithers off, leaving behind a twisting trail. *The Jungle Book* is alive and well.

OFF-BEAT SAFARIS

Rural Rajasthan is at the heart of a tourist revolution as more and more opportunities arise to get out of the cities, into the villages, hills and deserts, to camp under the stars, or stay in village forts, travelling by jeep, horse and camel. Prices and comfort levels vary enormously. Ask around, find out exactly what you are getting before you book, and don't allow yourselves to be swayed by high pressure sales techniques. Essential supplies include a hat, sun-block, water bottle and lip salve, and for overnight trips, a long-sleeved shirt, mosquito repellent, torch and sleeping bag. It can get very cold at night in the desert.

Bikaner

Bikaner is way out in the desert, with dunes in easy reach. It is not yet as well known as Jaisalmer for its camel safaris, but there are still plenty on offer, and still relatively undisturbed by other travellers.

Camelman
Opposite Sophia School, Jaipur Rd.
Tel: (0151) 2231244.

Rajasthan Safaris and Treks

Bassi House, Purani Ginani.
Tel: (0151) 2525594.
Vino Desert Safari
Opposite Gopeshwar Temple.
Tel: (0151) 2204445.

Jaisalmer

Every second person in Jaisalmer offers camel safaris. What most people do is a gentle little trip to the Sam Dunes, about 40km from town. Here, along with scores of other travellers during the season, you ride a camel up the dunes, followed by little boys selling cold drinks. At the top, you dismount, watch the sunset, then solemnly ride down again. Hardier options include rugged trips lasting several days, sleeping under the desert stars, along with the small desert wildlife.

Sahara Travels
Jeep and camel safaris. The company is best known for its owner, 'Mr Desert', winner for several years of the Desert Festival men's beauty pageant, and now a known face on advertising posters for the region.
First Fort Gate.
Tel: (02992) 52609.

SPECIAL ATRACTIONS.

CAMEL SAFARI JEEP TOUR
IN TRADITIONAL STYLE
Free General Information's
TRAIN BUS AIR TICKETS

CAMELS

Camels are crucial to the economy of the desert, a source of food (both milk and meat), transport, and clothing, and even a symbol of wealth. You can buy one whole and alive, or in a multitude of guises from *pattus* (huge camel wool shawls), and camel wool seats, to camel hide jars and water bottles, hats or slippers, paintings, and even toy camels made from camel skin. There are two distinct types of camels in Rajasthan. Jaisalmer riding camels are smaller and swifter, standing about 2.2m high, weighing about 550kg. Bikaneri camels are the workhorses, 2.6m tall, weighing about 680kg. Both can travel 35 to 40km a day.

Jodhpur

Several companies offer village safaris in the surrounding countryside – a rich mix of the eco-friendly Bishnoi settlements, camellers' homes, and the *dhurrie* weavers of Salawas. By far the most entertaining are those run by the maharaja's eccentric uncle, Swaroop Singh, owner of the enchanting Ajit Bhawan Hotel. Small groups are taken out by jeep to a wide variety of villages.
Ajit Bhawan Palace Hotel, near Circuit House, Airport Rd. Tel: (0291) 510410.

Shekhawati

The head office for a great number of camel and village safaris in the Shekhawati region of central Rajasthan is based in a restored 200-year-old palace, the Shahpura Palace, still maintained by the local ruling family.

Short, day safaris are also organised from Mandawa.
65km north from Jaipur on the Delhi road. Details and booking: Shahpura Guesthouse, D-257 Devi Marg, Bani Park, Jaipur 302 016. Tel: (0141) 2202293. Hotel Castle Mandawa. Tel: (01592) 223124; fax: (01592) 223171.

Udaipur
Aravalli Safari
*Sheetla Marg Lake Palace Rd.
Tel: (0294) 420282; fax: (0294) 420121.*

Camel safaris offer a novel, if bumpy experience

ART AND ARCHITECTURE
Samode

Samode, nestling in the Aravallis, is a little gem of Rajput architecture and style. It was built by a prime minister of the Jaipur state in the late-19th century, and has been sensitively restored by present members of the family. The picture-perfect uppermost level has the **Durbar Hall**, **Sheesh Mahal** and **Sultan Mahal** surrounding a beautiful courtyard. Even more breathtaking are the mirrorwork, paintings and murals that almost completely cover the surfaces of these rooms. Samode is a fabulous luxury hotel, and nearby, the **Samode Bagh** has been developed for tented accommodation in pavilion-like tents that authentically recapture the opulent Mughal style of living.

42km northwest from Jaipur on the way to Shekhawati. Tourist Information Office: Tel: (01423) 240013/4. Open: to residents and guests only.

Shekhawati

The little known area of Shekhawati, filling the gap between Bikaner, Jaipur and Alwar, was originally a province of Jaipur. It takes its name from Rao Shekha (1433–88) who declared independence from Jaipur in 1471. The kingdom never grew to rival its magnificent neighbours, has no major cities, and of its numerous smaller forts and palaces, only a few are significant. It was home, however, to a remarkable band of Marwari merchants who followed the money when the trade routes shifted from the desert camel

Brightly painted *havelis* are the hallmark of the Shekhawati region

An art gallery brings Indian creativity to the public

caravans to the sea. From the mid-18th to mid-20th centuries, they made vast fortunes which they spent on building grand *havelis* in their home towns and villages. Some of them are among the most important industrialist families in India today.

The typical three- to five-storey Rajasthani *haveli* (literally 'enclosed space') follows a pattern familiar from India's great Mughal palaces. Inward facing, it has blind walls and formidable gates to shut out the world, shaded colonnades to block the ferocious sun, and a cool, breezy water-filled central courtyard as a place of relaxation. The highlight of the Shekhawati *havelis* is, however, their wall paintings – images from an urban and Western culture newly introduced to their enterprising owners. Aeroplanes, gramophones, brass bands and colonial society ladies mingle with caparisoned elephants, gods and goddesses. You will also find wonderfully vivid frescoes in some of the temples and memorial *chhatris*. Fresco painting continued until about 1930, and the style evolved continuously. The most interesting towns in the region include Jhunjhunu, Dundlod, Mandawa, Nawalgarh, Ramgarh, Bissau and Fatehpur.

Tourist Information Office: Jaipur. Tel: (0141) 202586. The only really satisfactory way to tour is by car/taxi available in Jaipur for a 3-day, 2-night tour. Several local palaces have been turned into very comfortable, and often expensive, small hotels, most of which offer village and desert tours by jeep, camel or horse (check in Mandawa, Jhunjhunu, Dundlod, Nawalgarh). Other accommodation options are scarce and spartan.

Shopping

Shopping is one of the highlights of a trip to Delhi, Agra and Rajasthan, where retail outlets from sophisticated urban boutiques to vibrant local bazaars tempt even the most resistant traveller with their colour, variety, and challenge to bargaining skills. India's traditional crafts survive despite the preference of many for machine-made goods or those made of synthetic materials. There is a wealth of textiles and objects to captivate your senses.

Terracotta toys and bowls are beautiful and useful

How to shop
Part of the experience of shopping is to soak in the atmosphere without getting hassled by the crowds. Gauge the price range, and don't be swayed into parting with your money, however persistent or charming someone is, until you are ready. You are surrounded by some of the finest salesmen in the world and it is very hard to resist. In local bazaars and smaller shops, bargaining is essential. Don't believe anyone who says the post and packing will be free; don't get sucked into any dubious resale schemes, however plausible; and assume that all 'antiques' are fake. If genuine, they should have a certificate of authenticity, and you will need customs' clearance before you can export them. If you are buying something expensive and having it posted, pay by credit card so you are insured if it doesn't turn up.

What to buy
Carpets
A close second to those of Iran or Kashmir, luxuriant, close-knotted silk and wool pile carpets are best found in Jaipur and Delhi. Bikaner specialises in cheap and cheerful *namdahs* (felt rugs with embroidery), and brightly coloured cotton-weave *dhurries* are widely made in eastern Rajasthan and around Agra.

Jewellery
There is costume jewellery aplenty, from bright bangles and beads of lac, enamel and glass, to gorgeous, heavy tribal designs in silver and semi-precious stones. There is also a thriving market in loose gems, and superbly crafted gold jewellery in both Western and Indian designs. Prices for genuine articles are very reasonable but, unless you are knowledgeable, or have someone with you who is, be very, very careful. *(See also pp156–7.)*

Miniature paintings
Genuine miniatures are highly priced and rare to find, but there are superb reproductions both on paper and silk, available for a quarter the price. Use a magnifying glass to look at the detail of the brushstrokes. *(See also pp134–5.)*

Pottery

The best pottery around is charming Jaipur blue ware, made from fuller's earth, quartz and sodium sulphite. Traditional designs once used only blues, turquoise and white, but some greens, yellows and browns are now creeping in. Every village and region also has its own style of terracotta pots, bowls and images.

Stonework

Agra has a thriving tradition of *pietra dura* – beautifully crafted, delicate inlay of semi-precious stones (now usually fake) on marble. Numerous factory shops sell plates, trays and even tables, as well as cheaper work on soapstone. At Fatehpur Sikri, some 1,500 people make their living carving 'pregnant' elephants (with carved babies inside their trellised stomachs), frogs, and other animals, as well as small utility items of soapstone.

Textiles

Go to Jaipur for tie-dye and hand-block prints on cotton, linen and delicate fabrics such as mull; Jaisalmer for rich mirrored embroidery, patchwork and appliqué; and to Bikaner for heavy, coarse weaves of rough wool. Also look for superb Kashmiri wool jackets, shawls and stoles available in Delhi, Agra and Jaipur at very reasonable prices. *(See also pp156–7.)*

Other buys

Puppets and other decorative toys; leatherwork, from camel skin bags to embroidered slippers; embossed and/or enamelled brassware (the finest work is based on silver and even gold); light cotton quilts; wall hangings; carved wooden tables and chairs; essential oils, made up to your own recipe; spices; books (on India, but also cheap English-language editions)… the list is endless.

Puppets have a distinguished history here – and are also great gifts

Where to buy

The easiest way to shop is to head for a state-run emporium or hotel shopping mall, where you should be reasonably certain that prices are fair, and your silk is not polyester, or your carpet of nylon. However, do be very careful because most shops calling themselves government emporia and other official-sounding names are actually privately owned. The **Rajasthali** chain is managed by the Rajasthan Tourism Development Corporation, and every state in India has an official outlet in Delhi. Among the cities, Delhi, Jaipur and Jaisalmer offer excellent shopping opportunities.

More fun are the *karkhanas* (factory shops), where you can see anything from painting to inlay work, weaving to enamel in production. These are worth a visit even if you are not looking to buy. Remember that anywhere you are taken by a driver or guide will involve a commission – anything from 5 per cent to 20 per cent. On the other hand, some of them know of very good places that you could never find on your own. India has markets in abundance, with open-air market stalls selling fruit and vegetables, spices and dyes, fabric and shoes. Around every temple is a cluster of stalls selling coconuts and marigolds, strings of jasmine, and incense sticks as offerings to the gods. You need a zip replaced or a shoe mended? Turn your head and a *mochi* (shoemaker) will be waiting, cross-legged under a tree, needle in hand.

Best of all are the Old City bazaars, their endless narrow streets and alleys of tiny, dark, cubbyhole shops filled with the glitter of gold, the slither of crimson silk, and the sizzle of boiling oil. The air is pungent with *attar* (perfumed oil) of roses, with cardamom, garlic, incense (and often stale urine). Eager shopkeepers hurl bolt after bolt of fabric, carpet after carpet, that come sailing through the air in a glorious rainbow of colour and texture. Strings of beads cluster plumply in doorways, great stacks of globular cooking pots gleam dimly from the shadows, sculptures of marble and soapstone, sandalwood and bronze squat on heavily laden shelves. From every doorway comes the cry, 'You want ..? Just look ..!' – it's hard to resist.

One of the many market stalls with tempting trinkets

DELHI
Books
Connaught Place and Khan Market have the widest range of bookshops.
Bahri Sons
Khan Mkt.
Tel: (011) 2469 4610.
The Bookshop
Khan Mkt.
Tel: (011) 2469 7102.
The Bookworm
B-29 Connaught Place.
Tel: (011) 2332 2260.

Handicrafts and fabric
Government emporia and private shops stock a rich variety of handicrafts.
Cottage Industries (CCIE)
Fabric, jewellery, toys, furniture, decorative objects.
Corner of Janpath and Tolstoy Marg.
Tel: (011) 2332 1909.
Crafts Museum Shop
Crafts Museum, Pragati Maidan.
Tel: (011) 2337 1353.
Dastkaar
A crafts institution set up to cut out the middleman from crafts retailing.
Shahpur Jat.
Tel: (011) 2649 5920.
Fabindia
Handwoven linen, garments, rugs.
N Block Mkt, Greater

Kailash I.
Tel: (011) 2621 1032.
Khadi Gramodyog Bhavan
Handspun fabric, rugs, and crafts.
24 Regal Building, corner of Baba Kharak Marg and Connaught Circus.
Tel: (011) 2336 2231.
Tibet House
Tibetan crafts, books and clothes.
Lodi Rd.
Tel: (011) 2461 1515.

Good shopping areas
Baba Kharak Singh Marg
All the different states of India have crafts emporia strung along this road.
Near Connaught Place and Janpath.
Chandni Chowk
Old Delhi's main shopping area for the last 350 years. Good for perfume, jewellery and carpets.
Connaught Place
The whole area is filled with street stalls as well as regal, old established shops.
Dilli Haat
A custom-built crafts village run by Delhi Tourism, with regular stall changes and regional food for hassle-free tourist shopping.

Opposite INA Mkt, Aurobindo Marg.
Tel: (011) 2611 9055.
Hauz Khas Village
Up-market selection of designer boutiques.
Near Deer Park, Hauz Khas.
Janpath
Good souvenirs in the Tibetan Market.
Santushti Shopping Arcade
Boutique shopping arcade.
Opp Samrat Hotel, Chanakyapuri.
Tel: (011) 2467 9218.
Shahpur Jat
Designer outlets here sell garments, linen, antique and new carpets, and silver jewellery.
Off Siri Fort Rd.
Sunder Nagar Market
A growing showcase for fine furniture, jewellery and real antiques.
Opposite Hotel Oberoi.

A whole raft of daily markets shifts around the city. The best example is the Sunday flea market, beside the Red Fort. Excellent for out-of-print and used books.

AGRA
Agra does not have the variety of Delhi or Jaipur. Be prepared for some

Antiques and their reproductions for sale

heavy bargaining. Don't take things on trust, and arrange to have them shipped. Insist on bills, and a copy of all the necessary paperwork.

UP Handicraft Palace Complex
Two shops have a wide range of products, from carpets, garments to *pietra dura* inlay.
49 Bansal Nagar.
Tel: (0562) 368214.

The best shopping areas are beside the entrance to the Taj Mahal, to Mahatma Gandhi Road, and to Gwalior Road. Also, at Sadar Bazaar, Kinari Bazaar and Pratap Pura.

BIKANER
Abhivyakti
Outlet for the **Urmul Trust**, a non-government organisation, working with craftspersons.

Beautiful, ethnic weave fabrics, shawls, cushion covers and other linen.
Inside Junagarh Fort.

JAIPUR
Anokhi
Wonderful hand-printed clothes, soft furnishings and accessories. Home base of an international designer chain, with much lower prices than outlets abroad.
2 Tilak Marg, behind Secretariat.
Tel: (0141) 2381619.
(See also Delhi, tel: (011) 2688 3076.)
Bhuramal Rajmal Surana
For the rich. Superbly made traditional Indian jewellery, dripping with precious stones.
Lal Katra, Johari Bazaar.
Tel: (0141) 2560628/ 561440.
Channi Carpets and Textiles
One of several fine carpet factories in the area; guided tours and a showroom.
Mount Rd, opposite Ramgarh Rd.
Handloom Haveli
Several outlets for hand-woven fabrics under one roof.
Lalpura House, Sansar Chandra Rd.

Omdain
Fine, traditional gold and silver jewellery.
228–9 Johari Bazaar.
Tel: (0141) 2560489.
Rajasthali
Government emporium with wide range of fixed-price souvenirs.
Ajmeri Gate, MI Rd.
Tel: (0141) 2367176.

The whole of the old city is effectively one massive market. Try Ramganj Bazaar (handmade and embroidered leather footwear); Badi Chaupar, Johari Bazaar, Jadiyon-ka-

Elaborate textiles and embroidery are a Rajasthani speciality, cheap and portable

Rasta, Gopalji-ka-Rasta, Haldiyon-ka-Rasta (jewellery); Maniharon-ka-Rasta, off Tripolia Bazaar (lac bangles); Khajanewalon-ka-Rasta, off Chandpol Bazaar (stone carving); Hawa Mahal area (real and fake antiques, and feather-light quilts; Johari Bazaar (textiles). For the finest block prints and handmade paper, head for Sanganer, 16km southwest of Jaipur.

JAISALMER
Central Jaisalmer is one huge souvenir shop, in particular, areas by the Fort Gate, around the Jain temples, and near the *havelis.* Shops inside the *havelis* are expensive.
Rajasthali and **Khadi Bhandar** are both just outside Amar Sagar Gate.

JODHPUR
Abbani Handicraft
High Court Rd, near Tourist Bungalow.
Lucky Silk Palace
Sojari Gate.
Mohanlal Verhomal
Wonderful spice shop, also sells outside the Fort Gate and by mail order.
Shop No. 209B, Vegetable Mkt, Clock Tower.
Tel: (0291) 615846.

Rajasthan Art Emporium
One of a strip of enticing antique shops.
Umaid Bhavan Palace Rd.
Rajasthan Khadi Sangathan
BK ka Bagh.

Emporia cluster around Sojari Gate, and factory shops around Siwanchai and Jalori Gates.
Markets include Sardar Bazaar, Clock Tower, Station Road (jewellery), Tripolia Bazaar (crafts), Khanda Falsa (tie-dye), Lakhara Bazaar (lac bangles) and Mochi Bazaar (shoes).

UDAIPUR
Jagdish Emporium
A range of handicrafts and fine textiles.
City Palace Rd.
Rajasthali
Fixed-price government emporium.
Chetak Circle.

Good souvenir shopping areas include Chetak Circle, Hathi Pol (the outer court of the City Palace), Palace Road and Shastri Circle. Markets include Bapu Bazaar, Clock Tower, Nehru Bazaar, Sindhi Bazaar, Bada Bazaar.

Against a background of dusty land and sun-bleached skies, Rajasthan is filled with opulent colour, the sparkle of mirror and silver and precious stones, the shimmer of silk and a vivid kaleidoscope of cotton.

Tribal jewellery is mainly silver, copper, and bronze, bold, beautiful and huge. Women literally wear the family silver in a jangle of necklaces and clatter of bangles, with ivory or bone bracelets on the upper arm to show their married status. There are two traditions of classical jewellery. Jazzy *kundan* work is the art of setting small stones, jewels, or crystals in a complex pattern of 24-carat gold. *Meenakari* is the art of enamelling, etched into a base metal, or in the case of jewellery, gold. The finest pieces combine both, the front bright with shining stones, the back a perfectly crafted enamel mosaic.

Perhaps even more fabulous are the fabrics. The men are usually responsible

for weaving, dyeing and tailoring the cloth, and for the sumptuous gold *zardozi* embroidery used on festive saris. The women handle the delicate tying of knots for gaudy *bandhani* work – infinitely intricate tie-dye, with pin-head wisps of material tightly bound and rebound to create complex patterns of dots, circles, squares and stripes. They also do the elaborate embroidery and appliqué which covers their bodices and waistcoats with heavy patterns and shining mirror fragments. Traditional dyes were derived from iron and indigo, jasmine, pistachio, saffron and mulberry; these days they are usually chemical. Shot cottons are woven with a warp and weft of different colours, while the

Alwar area specialises in dyeing the front and back of the cloth in different hues, and Sanganer, just outside Jaipur, is famous for its hand-block prints, using carved wooden blocks as templates. The materials are familiar in Europe.

Eighteenth-century noblemen's *bandhani* handkerchiefs gave their name to the bandana, while women decked themselves out in sprigged muslin – the finest block printed cottons. Carpets and rugs woven mainly in Jaipur and Jodhpur, also display the Rajasthani eye for colour. Today, Rajasthani textiles and jewellery are at the forefront of the ethnic revolution which dominates the catwalks of apparel designers around the world.

Tie-dye, embroidery, weaves, heavy silver and fragile gold filigree – local crafts are thriving and exquisite

E n t e r t a i n m e n t

Cinema ranks as the most popular form of entertainment for Indians, with the Mumbai film industry the largest in the world. Night life is meagre, confined to the really large urban centres, with a smattering of classical music and dance, and theatre. Performances increase during the cooler months. Rural India, however, sings with folk drama, music, dance and puppet shows – each region with its own particular style of performance.

India makes more films a year than Hollywood

DELHI

Delhi has all the entertainment you could hope for in a major international city. What is not produced locally comes with international tours of everything from symphonies to rock. The country's national theatre repertory produces professional fare, mostly in Hindi, but there is a year-round calendar of good amateur Hindi and English plays. France, Italy, Britain, Germany and the USA all have cultural institutes with touring lectures and regular films. Some of the international hotels have discos or cabarets, at a price, and there are several venues for cultural programmes of Indian music and dance. As everywhere in India, there are numerous cinemas showing mainstream films in English, as well as a huge array of Hindi 'Bollywood' blockbusters. A useful weekly booklet, *Delhi Diary*, has full entertainment listings and lots of other up-to-date tourist and practical information. It is readily available at all hotels and bookshops.

Auditoria and galleries

These are all multi-purpose cultural venues with a range of activities – lectures, dance, theatre and music.

Habitat Centre
Lodi Road.
Tel: (011) 2464 9907.
Indian Council for Cultural Relations
Azad Bhawan,
Indraprastha Estate.
Tel: (011) 2331 2274.

India International Centre
Max Mueller Marg.
Tel: (011) 2461 9431.
Kamani Auditorium
Copernicus Marg.
Tel: (011) 2388 8084.
National School of Drama
Bhawalpur House.
Tel: (011) 2338 9769.
Siri Fort Auditorium
Siri Fort Road.
Tel: (011) 2649 3370.
Triveni Kala Sangam
205 Tansen Marg.
Tel: (011) 2371 8833.

Cultural programmes
Dances of India
Programme of classic, folk and tribal dances.
Anjuman Hall, Bahadur Shah Zafar Marg, near Delhi Gate.
Tel: (011) 2331 7831/2332 0968. Nightly 6.45pm.

Son et Lumière
Nightly tour of Mughal
history, set in the Red
Fort grounds.
*Red Fort. Tel: (011) 2600
121, ext 2156, (011) 2274
4580 after 5pm. In Hindi
and English. Times vary
according to season.
Admission charge.*

Discos and bars
Djinns
*Hyatt Regency Hotel,
Bhikaji Cama Place,
Ring Rd.
Tel: (011) 2679 1234.*
Ghungroo
*Maurya Sheraton Hotel,
Diplomatic Enclave,
Chanakyapuri.
Tel: (011) 2301 0101.*
Ricks
*Taj Mansingh Hotel,
Mansingh Rd.
Tel: (011) 2301 6162.*

ELSEWHERE
Options drop off
dramatically outside
Delhi, although you will
still find at least one
cultural programme, and
several cinemas, in any
large town. The best way
to occupy yourself in the
evenings is to head for
the markets which buzz
with excitement. It is also
where you are most likely
to find any street
entertainers.

AGRA
Taj Khema
Nightly folk dance and
music programme
presented in the
restaurant garden, with
views of the Taj Mahal.
*Eastern Gate, Taj Rd.
Tel: (0562) 2230001.*

JAIPUR
Jawahar Kala Kendra
Music, dance and
puppetry in an open-air
theatre.
*Jawaharlal Nehru Marg.
Tel: (0141) 2510501.*
**Rajputana Palace
Sheraton**
Nightly performance of
music, dance and
puppetry in an open-air
theatre in the hotel
gardens, 7–9pm.
*Palace Rd.
Tel: (0141) 2360011.*
Ravindra Manch
*Jawaharlal Nehru Marg.
Tel: (0141) 2669061.*

JODHPUR
**Ghoomar Tourist
Bungalow**
*High Court Rd.
Tel: (0291) 244010.*
Sangeet Natak Academy
Folk dancing in high
season only.
*Paota 'B' Rd. Details
available from the Tourist
Office.
Tel: (0291) 245083.*

Programmes also at Ajit
Bhavan and Umaid
Bhavan (*see pp168–9*).

UDAIPUR
**Bhartiya Lok Kala
Mandal**
Some of Rajasthan's
finest programmes with a
famous puppet troop and
regional dance and music.
*Near Chetak Circle.
Tel: (0294) 2529296. Daily
6–7pm. Admission charge.*
Lake Palace Hotel
Puppet shows at 6pm,
dances at 9pm daily, for
guests and diners only.
*Lake Pichola.
Tel: (0294) 2527961.*
Meera Kala Mandir
Nightly dance and music
performances.
*City Station Rd.
Tel: (0294) 2583176.
Mon–Sat 7–8pm.
Admission charge.*

Drums play an important role
in tribal music

Children

Although India has more children of its own than almost any other country in the world, this is not the ideal destination, especially for babies and small children, with very real health hazards (*see pp180–1*). Once into their teens, however, they should have built up enough stamina and natural immunity and the situation is very different.

A winning smile for the camera

Basic survival

Try and base yourself in one place, preferably in a good hotel with a swimming pool. The chef will normally be happy to make up fresh food to your instructions, with some warning, but take an emergency supply of bottled baby food anyway. Chips and biscuits, hard boiled eggs, bananas and bottled fizz are available everywhere and make up an adequate survival diet for slightly older children, if the worst comes to the worst. The hotel should be able to organise a competent babysitter for you. It is not really a good idea to hire your own nanny as most are uneducated women with very different standards of hygiene and safety to your own. Western brands of disposable nappies are freely available in Delhi. Do your sightseeing in relatively small chunks, and read up ahead of time, as the area is filled with wonderful legends and stories, sufficient to keep any child enthralled. Maintaining some sort of diary and/or collection will help focus their attention.

The biggest problems spring from kindness. Indians adore Western children. Your child will act as a magnet, with people crowding in close to see and touch. Never mind the cleanliness of the hands, most children hate being pawed or crowded. Kind Indian mothers will also feed your child unhygienic drinks or snacks, so you must be both vigilant and diplomatic. Finally, India is full of potential wonders for children, from fairground rides precariously held together, to streetsellers laden with simple, handcrafted toys not checked for toxicity. Book and toy shops are, however, laden with wonderful goods, both Indian and imported.

Things to do
Transport

Just getting around can be an adventure. Auto- and cycle-rickshaws will be great favourites, and trains will also be popular, especially if you can still find a last, lurking steam engine. In Jaipur, the elephant ride at Amber is thrilling.

In town

The forts are sufficiently dramatic to avoid becoming boring old museums, especially if you can find good details like the staggered gates designed to stop a charging elephant, or an infant maharaja's cradles and toys. Some temples, like the Karni Mata temple near

Bikaner with its sacred rats, provide better entertainment than others, but nobody seems to mind too much if your children play aeroplanes around the courtyard. The markets are lively, colourful, and noisy, and there is plenty of street entertainment with musicians and snake charmers and puppets. Where there are lakes, there are usually pedaloes and rowing boats, and every town has at least one good park with space for running, and shade for exhausted parents.

Out of town

Older children will probably enjoy a desert safari, whether by jeep, camel or horse, at least as much as you. Ranthambhore and Sariska offer tiger hunting (with a camera), while Bharatpur is not only fascinating for its birds, but allows you to walk in the bush and look for pythons.

In Delhi

Delhi has several specially designed attractions, such as **Bal Bhavan** and the **National Children's Museum and Aquarium** *1 Kotla Rd, tel: (011) 2331 4701, open: Tue–Sat 9am–1pm & 2–5pm; Aquarium 11am–5pm,* **Shankar's International Dolls Museum** *Bahadur Shah Zafar Marg,* **Zoological Gardens**, and the **Appu Ghar** fairground, both near Pragati Maidan.

Cricket is a national obsession, played on improvised pitches from street alleys to village *maidans* (open fields)

Sport and Leisure

Although few foreigners think of India as a sporting destination (with the exception, perhaps, of the mountain sports in the Himalayas), it does have almost everything on offer, from spectator sports to those mainly for the local middle and upper classes, who can afford to pay. Rajasthan, however, is not one of the best equipped regions in the country.

Indian wrestlers have enjoyed great success on the international stage

The traditional sports of the maharajas were hunting (now banned), military skills such as sword play (now, hopefully, not needed), and expensive pastimes like polo, and collecting vintage cars by the rich. Cricket, not football, is the national obsession. India also excels internationally in hockey, badminton, tennis and table tennis.

Adventure sports

At present, there are few adventure sports available in this region, other than a little gentle rock climbing near Delhi. Rajasthan is beginning to build up a programme, however, concentrating first on providing watersports such as windsurfing, sailing and waterskiing on some of the larger lakes, such as Jaisamand, 50km south of Udaipur. Rajasthan Tourism has set up an **Adventure Cell** in Jaipur (*tel: (0141) 2202586/2203531*).

Angling

Rajasthan offers several opportunities for fishing – at Bandh Baretha (near Bharatpur), Siliserh, Mansarovar (near Sariska), Ramgarh (Jaipur) and other lakes. Anglers are advised to carry their own equipment and obtain permission from the Fisheries Department.

Cricket

Cricket is the favoured game of little boys from villages and dusty city backstreets, and their fathers, who eagerly spend their hard-earned rupees to crowd into noisy matches. Great cricketers are heroes, as big as pop and movie stars, and test cricket has the stature of the FA Cup or Rosebowl.

Golf

Golf is beginning to catch on among businessmen and others, thanks to visiting expats (the Japanese in particular). Delhi has some fine courses and there are also courses in each of the main cities. Most are open to visitors.

Health and fitness

Many of the 5-star de luxe hotels have a Western-style gymnasium, sauna and Jacuzzi. Health and fitness activities are rapidly becoming popular, but Indian-style techniques are far more likely to involve Ayurvedic massage, herbal steam baths, yoga and meditation.

Polo

The polo season is nowhere near as frenetic as it was 50 years ago, but Delhi, Jaipur and Jodhpur all still have grounds on the international circuit. The polo-playing season lasts from November until March. Check local listings or with the tourist office for matches.

Swimming

There are very few public pools, and swimming in natural water is not really a good idea. Most 5-star hotels and sporting clubs have good pools, and many are prepared to open them up to non-residents for the payment of a fee.

DELHI CLUBS

Best Western Resort and Country Club

Beautiful setting in the Aravallis on the outskirts of Delhi. This is the first Jack Nicklaus course in South Asia. Also offers other sports facilities and activities for children.
NH8 to Gurgaon, southwest of Delhi. Tel: 91 1267 278202.

Delhi Golf Club

18 holes, 220 acres, 200 species of trees and shrubs, 300 species of birds, and numerous Lodi tombs and monuments. Casual membership and equipment hire available.
Dr Zakir Hussain Marg. Tel: (011) 2436 2235.

Delhi Polo Club

Casual membership, tickets for tournaments and information on polo throughout India.
President's Estate, Rashtrapati Bhavan. No telephone number available.

The Meadows Golf and Country Club

Delightful 18-hole golf course with excellent facilities, including cottage accommodation.
On the Gurgaon–Sohna Rd, 4km from the Gurgaon Roundabout. Office: F-4/7 Vasant Vihar. Tel: (0124) 2687 2274.

The Resort Country Club

Luxurious country club with great sports facilities in addition to children's entertainment such as pony and camel rides. Also a bar, restaurant, and cottage-style accommodation.
About 30km from Delhi, off the Jaipur Rd. Tel: (01267) 78202/5.

Delhi has several major sporting stadiums hosting a range of home-grown and international events. Check local listings and *Delhi Diary* (*see p158*).

India's test cricketers are national heroes

Food and Drink

Western foodies tend by nature to scorn the hotel dining rooms and try to hunt out the little backstreet bistro that no one else has discovered. In India, this can be a bad mistake. There are a few exceptions, but most of the really good restaurants are run by the hotels – and the Indians know it too. Here you will find not only the cream of cuisines, from Mughlai to South Indian, French or Thai, but lavish (and incredibly reasonable) lunchtime buffets, and 24-hour coffee shops for the chilli-weary palate. Only rarely will you find yourself in a tourist ghetto.

Bubbling cauldrons of Indian fast food

Once out of the rarified atmosphere of hotels, the average Indian restaurant has strip lighting, sticky formica table tops, a menu running to several pages with Indian, Chinese (second favourite) and Continental food. Indian cuisine can be some of the finest in the world (*see pp170–71*). Sadly, however, the good stuff is all cooked at home, behind closed doors, and what you are usually offered is difficult for non-Indians to digest. The menu lists hundreds of mouth-watering possibilities, all so heavily spiced and oily they taste the same. If there is no alternative, at least ensure that the food is freshly cooked by choosing a place that seems well frequented. Remember, it is always better to select from the many vegetarian options. Meat is almost always chicken or mutton (goat). It is forbidden for Hindus to eat beef (any steak will be buffalo), and pork is anathema to Muslims. Fish is best avoided in these inland areas.

So-called Continental food is a horrifying mix of multi-national institutional and England circa 1930s. Breakfast includes cornflakes or *dalia* (porridge) with boiling milk, greasy omelettes and fire-toasted bread. For lunch or dinner, noodles or spaghetti with a dollop of tomato ketchup-based sauce is a common offering, along with chips (known as finger chips to avoid confusion with crisps, which are also called chips).

Street eating

Normal travelling wisdom says avoid street stalls. However, some of India's most popular restaurants are streetside *dhabas*, with long trestle tables and bubbling cauldrons. They usually keep things simple, serving a basic *thali* (fixed menu and price) to everyone. The turnover is huge, so the food is always fresh, and you can watch it cooking to allay any lingering doubts. Indians prefer using their fingers to forks (right hand only; using the left is a grave social blunder). No matter where you eat, hygiene must be the first consideration (*see* Health, *p180*).

If you are not used to eating spicy foods regularly, don't expect to be able to survive a solid diet of chillies without trouble. There are non-hot options if you look, while simple foods such as plain rice, *chapatis* and yoghurt are excellent if you feel ill. Take a few muesli bars or biscuits as iron rations.

Drinks

Fizzy drinks, cartons of fruit juice, and bottled mineral water are freely available. Familiar names include Coke, Pepsi and Sprite. Local versions include Thums Up (cola), Fanta (orange) and

Limca (lemon). A refreshing alternative is fresh lime soda. Yoghurt-based *lassis* come sweet, plain or salted, and also help mop up the hottest spices. Weak instant coffee is usually available, but tea (*chai*) is more popular in north India. It normally comes with the milk and huge quantities of sugar all boiled in together. When you are ordering, specify that you want separate or 'tray' tea, that is, milk and tea served separately without sugar. Alcohol is served only in luxury hotels, rarely in ordinary restaurants. There are several varieties of beer and spirits (including imported brands) available in liquor shops, for a price.

Fizzy drinks and fresh fruit juice are sold along with hot snacks

Where to eat
Prices
The following categories are based on the cost of a full meal for one, without alcohol. It is possible to eat much more cheaply, for only a few rupees if you go to the street stalls and small cafés.

★   150–300 rupees
★★   300–500 rupees
★★★   up to 1,500 rupees

DELHI
Ansal Plaza ★
A shopping centre with a range of multi-cuisine restaurants. **Geoffries** (*tel: (011) 2626 1305*), and **The Buck Stops Here**, are both good.
Off Siri Fort Rd.

Basil & Thyme ★★
Light Continental in a shopping complex.
Santushti Complex.
Tel: (011) 2467 4933.

Chor Bizarre ★★
Excellent Kashmiri cuisine. Very convenient after the Red Fort Son et Lumière. Book ahead.
4/15 Asaf Ali Rd.
Tel: (011) 2327 3821.

Dhaba ★★★
Indian food well served.
Claridges Hotel.
Tel: (011) 2301 0211.

Flavours ★
Personal service by the Italian owner and chef.
Bank complex, Defence Colony.
Tel: (011) 2464 5644.

Karim's Nemat Kada ★★
Popular Old Delhi eatery with kebabs and Mughlai cuisine.
Matya Mahal, opp south gate of the Jama Masjid.
Tel: (011) 2326 4981. Also at Nizamuddin West.

New Friends Colony Community Centre ★★
Slightly out of the way but full of interesting places. **Ego** (*tel: (011) 2631 8185*), **Mezz** (*tel: (011) 2684 6644*), **Dawatkhana**, and others.

Nirula's ★
A travellers' institution, with good fast foods, and and other restaurants.
L Block, Connaught Place.
Tel: (011) 2332 2419.

The Rampur Kitchen ★★
North Indian specialities in a cheerful setting.
Khan Mkt.
Tel: (011) 2463 1222.

The Village Bistro ★★/★★★
A huge complex of multi-cuisine restaurants, and a rooftop barbecue overlooking the Hauz Khas ruins. Live entertainment and shopping on tap.
12 Hauz Khas Village, near Deer Park.
Tel: (011) 2685 3857/ 2685 2226.

AGRA
Garden View Restaurant ★
Indian, Italian, Mexican and Continental food.
Hotel Sakura, 48 Old Idgah Colony, near Idgah Bus Stand.
Tel: (0562) 2369793.

Nauratna ★★★
Mughlai restaurant in a palace-style hotel.
Mughal Sheraton, Fatehabad Rd, Taj Ganj.
Tel: (0562) 2361701.

Drinks on the lawn, Jai Mahal Hotel, Jaipur

Novotel Brasserie ★★
Part of a French-based
chain offering Indian and
Continental food.
Tajnagri Scheme,
Fatehabad Rd.
Tel: (0562) 2368282.

Only Restaurant ★
Garden restaurant run by
former Sheraton staff.
45 Taj Rd, Crossing Phool
Sayed. Tel: (0562) 2364333.

Taj Khema ★★
A range of food, good
views of the Taj Mahal,
and entertainment.
Eastern Gate, Taj Rd.
Tel: (0562) 2330140.

AJMER
Honey Dew Restaurant ★
Cheap and cheerful, with
Indian and Continental
food.
Opp the railway station.

Hotel Mansingh
Palace ★★
Good coffee shop and
dining room.
Vaishali Nagar, over-
looking the lake.
Tel: (0145) 2425956.

ALWAR
Hotel Sariska Palace ★★
Multi-cuisine in a con-
verted former palace/
hunting lodge.
Opp the Sariska Park

5-STAR RESTAURANTS, DELHI
Ashok *Tel: (011) 2611 0101.*
Durbar (North Indian); Tokyo
(Japanese).
Hyatt Regency
Tel: (011) 2679 1234.
La Piazza (Italian), TK's
(Oriental meat and fish grills).
Imperial
Tel: (011) 2334 1234.
Spice Route (Spicy Asian
from India to Indonesia).
Maurya Sheraton
Tel: (011) 2611 2233.
Dum Pukht (Mughlai, on

slow heat in earthen vessels);
Bukhara (Tandoori);
Bali Hi (Polynesian).
Oberoi *Tel: (011) 2436 3030.*
Kandahar (North West
Frontier); La Rochelle
(Continental); Ban Thai (Thai).
Taj Mansingh
Tel: (011) 2302 6162.
House of Ming (Chinese).
Taj Palace
Tel: (011) 2334 1234.
Handi (Indian); Orient Express
(French *nouvelle cuisine*).

entrance, 35km from Alwar.
Tel: (0144) 2841322.

BHARATPUR
Forest Lodge ★
Pleasant ITDC-run hotel
and simple restaurant,
best in Bharatpur.
Inside the bird sanctuary.
Tel: (05644) 222760.

BIKANER
Amber ★
Indian vegetarian food.
Station Rd.
Tel: (0151) 523863.

Chotoo Matoo ★
Indian vegetarian food.
Station Rd.
Tel: (0151) 220 1122.

Thar Hotel ★
Veg and non-veg Indian
food, considered to be the
best in town.
Near Ambedkar Circle.
No telephone.

Lalgarh Palace ★★★
Bikaner's only five-star
hotel in a former
palace (*see p80*) with
a suitably grand
restaurant and live
entertainment.
Palace Rd, about 3km
north of town centre.
Tel: (0151) 2540201.

CHITTORGARH
Morcha Restaurant ★
Pleasant and ordinary, the
best option in town.
Hotel Pratap Palace,
Sri Gurukul Rd, opp GPO.
Tel: (01472) 240099.

KOTA
Brijraj Bhavan Palace ★★
A wonderful old royal
palace, this is Kota's
best hotel and restaurant
by a long way. Residents
only.
Civil Lines.
Tel: (0744) 2450529.

Palace View Garden Restaurant ★
Open-air vegetarian restaurant with north and south Indian, Chinese and Continental food.
Near Palace, Barrage Rd.

JAIPUR
Chandralok ★★
Traditional Rajasthani food in pleasant surroundings.
MI Rd, above Lakshmi Commercial Bank.

LMB (Lakshmi Mishthan Bhandar) ★
Right in the centre of the old town. Good, cheap vegetarian food.
Johari Bazaar.
Tel: (0141) 2565844.

Niro's ★★★
Widely regarded as the best non-hotel restaurant in Jaipur and popular with locals. Normal menu of Indian, Continental, and Chinese food.
MI Rd. Tel: (0141) 2374493.

Rambagh Palace ★★★
Built by Ram Singh II, this superb palace, home of later maharajas, was the only private residence in the world with its own polo ground. It is now Jaipur's grandest hotel.

Come here for a drink at least, if not to eat the excellent food.
Bhavani Singh Rd.
Tel: (0141) 2381919.

Other hotels with good dining rooms include *(area code 0141)*: the Jai Mahal (*tel: 2371616*), Rajputana Palace Sheraton (*tel: 2401140*), Hotel Man Singh (*tel: 2378771*) (all ★★★) and the Gangaur Tourist Bungalow (*tel: 2371641*, ★).

JAISALMER
Golden Fort ★
Cheap and cheerful Indian and Continental food. Roof terrace with fort view and live music.
Hanuman Chouraha, off Collector's Office Rd, near the Tourist Bungalow.
Tel: (02992) 252545.

Gorbandh Palace ★
Coffee shop and two restaurants.
1 Tourist Complex, Sam Rd. Tel: (02992) 251511.

Hotel Dhola Maru ★
A Rajasthan Tourism hotel. The food here is wonderful. Phone ahead to place your order.
Jethwai Rd, 4km out of town. Tel: (02992) 252863.

Monica ★
Popular with travellers, offers a good Rajasthani *thali*.
Near 1st Fort Gate.

Trio ★
Light, bright, and popular, cheap rooftop terrace, with good Indian and Continental food.
Above Bank of Baroda, Gandhi Chowk, near Amar Sagar Gate.
Tel: (02992) 252733.

Vyas Meal Service ★
Authentic vegetarian cuisine.
Inside Citadel, near Jain temples.

JODHPUR
Ajit Bhawan Palace ★★
One-sitting dinner at 7pm each evening in the palace courtyard, with dancers and musicians as well as good food and company. Book ahead.
Near Circuit House, Airport Rd.
Tel: (0291) 2511410.

Fort View ★
Rooftop vegetarian restaurant which lives up to its name.
Govind Hotel, Station Rd, Opp the GPO.
Tel: (0291) 222758.

An outdoor feast, Ajit Bhawan, Jodhpur

food is definitely good.
*Set back from road, near
petrol station.
Tel: (02974) 238391.*

RANTHAMBHORE
**Sawai Madhopur
Lodge ★★**
Former royal hunting
lodge. Attractive garden,
bar and restaurant.
*About 5km from Sawai
Madhopur, on the
Ranthambhore road.
Tel: (07462) 220541.*

UDAIPUR
Berry's ★
Simple restaurant with
good Indian, Chinese
and Continental food.
*Chetak Circle.
Tel: (0294) 2419927.*

Lake Palace Hotel ★★★
Excellent lunchtime
buffet and à la carte
dinners (Indian and
Continental) in splendid
surroundings with live
entertainment.
*Lake Pichola.
Tel: (0294) 2528800.*

Frigo ★
Popular, cheap and
cheerful fast food joint.
*Sardarpura.
Tel: (0291) 233212.*

Kalinga ★/★★
Popular travellers'
hangout with regional
and Continental food.
*Hotel Adarsh Niwas, Opp
the station.
Tel: (0291) 2627338.*

Umaid Bhavan ★★★
Jodhpur's top hotel has a
formal restaurant with an
excellent lunchtime buffet
and a coffee shop.
*See also p116.
Umaid Bhavan Rd.
Tel: (0291) 2510101.*

MOUNT ABU
Hotel Hilltone ★
Not as pretty as some of
the palace hotels, but the

Shilpi ★
Open-air restaurant
serving all types of food,
near the Shilpgram and
Lake Fateh Sagar. Public
access swimming pool.
*Rani Rd.
Tel: (0294) 2560635.*

The word 'curry' has three possible variations: the Tamil word for sauce is *kari*; the *kari* leaf is a commonly used spice; and there is a north Indian dish, made with chickpea flour and buttermilk, called *karhi*. Curry as a dish was an invention of the Raj, however, and has nothing to do with real Indian food. The spice base used for proper Indian cooking is a *masala* paste, with a different mix of ingredients for each dish. Common spices include chilli, cloves, turmeric, cardamom, fenugreek, cinnamon, cumin, garlic, mace, nutmeg, coriander, tamarind, poppy seeds, saffron, caraway, ginger, peppercorns, asafoetida, mustard and *kari* leaf. Contrary to all popular belief, not all Indian food is laden with chillies, although most dishes are highly flavoured. Even Indians would never expect to survive a *vindaloo*-strength blast every day.

Every region of India has its own distinctive cuisine. In Delhi you will find them all, and more. Some favourite dishes, such as South Indian *dosas* and *idlis*, the Mughal *biryani* and Punjabi *tandoori*, the Raj's peppery mulligatawny soup, the sweet Bengali *ras malai,* and the *kulfi*, Indian ice cream, have become industry standards found in restaurants throughout India and the world.

On the whole, north India eats more meat than the south, while the carbohydrates are provided by a range of wheat-based breads, such as *naan*, *roti*, *paratha* and *puri*, rather than a constant diet of rice. Mughlai cuisine is the finest and richest on offer. The culinary legacy of the Mughal court, it blends Persian and Indian dishes and the very best of ingredients, cooking with yoghurt, almonds, raisins and butter to create rich, luscious, creamy sauces and delicately perfumed rice. It is rarely very hot. Marinated and grilled meat and vegetable kebabs are typically Muslim. Dry *tandoori*, again marinated and cooked in a clay oven, only arrived in Delhi from the Northwest Frontier after Partition in 1947, but has been enthusiastically adopted. Traditional Rajasthani food, with breads and spicy vegetarian dishes, can be hard to find.

Puddings are not a standard part of the normal menu, but do exist. Most are milk-based and immensely sweet. *Halva*-type sweets are made to celebrate festivals. They are elaborately decorated, even with wafer-thin sheets of real, edible silver and gold. Meals are usually ended with a mouth freshener and digestive, such as aniseed or *pan*, a cocktail of betel nut and flavourings such as cloves, cardamom, fennel, lime, or the red catechu bark, all served in a heart-shaped betel leaf.

Bread, vegetables and spices are the most important ingredients used for north Indian cooking

MENU READER

Betel nut – mildly intoxicating nut chewed after meals

Biryani – mixed dish of mildly spiced rice, vegetables, and sometimes meat

Chai – tea boiled with milk and sugar

Chapati – simple, griddle-baked unleavened bread

Dahi – yoghurt

Daal – dish made of lentils, with a consistency ranging from thin soup to a thick purée, served with most meals

Dosa – large rice flour pancake

Idlis – dumplings of fermented rice flour

Kheema – minced meat

Koftas – meat or vegetable balls

Kulfi – ice cream, flavoured with pistachio and cardamom

Lassi – thin yoghurt drink

Murg – chicken

Naan – baked, leavened bread, usually eaten with *tandoori*

Pan – leaf-wrapped package of aromatic palate cleansers and betel nut

Panir – a soft cheese

Paratha – bread, layered with butter and sometimes stuffed with meat and/or vegetables

Raita – side dish of yoghurt with mint, cucumber or onion

Tandoori – dry meats and vegetables, marinated and oven grilled

Thali – full set meal of rice, *daal* and several meat or vegetable dishes

Hotels and Accommodation

People build great hotels in India; it's maintaining them that's the problem. No one seems to notice as the dust builds up, and the cockroaches start nesting. As a result, the industry is definitely two-tier, with a top class of superbly run international standard hotels – and everything else. The trick of living well at an affordable price is knowing where's good this season, or even this month. The good news is that Rajasthan definitely has more than its fair share of good hotels and guesthouses, and the sophistication of Western requirements is beginning to rub off.

A gigantic board of traditional chessmen at the Jai Vilas Hotel, Jaipur

Up-market hotels

The service in high-quality hotels is impeccable. You will also get a marble bathroom, 24-hour room service, satellite TV, messenger services, shopping arcades, travel agents, gyms, beauty salons, a swimming pool, and anything else you can think of. In Delhi, there are custom-built business hotels, with fully functional secretarial services, conference facilities, and so on. Elsewhere, businessmen are catered for by the 5-star de luxe tourist hotels which offer all the service, most of the facilities, and much more atmosphere. Rates are calculated in US dollars, and there is an extra 10 per cent luxury tax.

Lake Palace Hotel, Udaipur

CENTRAL BOOKING
Between them, these chains own almost all the luxury and mid-range hotels in the region.

ITDC
The state-run chain of the India Tourism Development Corporation (ITDC), with hotels in Delhi, Agra, Bharatpur, Jaipur and Udaipur. They come in three types – dirt cheap and dirty; mid-range, reasonable price and very comfortable; and all-singing all-dancing super-luxury. Check which you are booking.
Jeevan Vihar, 3rd Fl, 3 Sansad Marg, New Delhi 110 001. *Tel: (011) 373 5557.*

Oberoi Hotels
Luxury and mid-range hotels in Delhi, Jaipur and Agra.
c/o Oberoi Hotel, Dr Zakir Hussain Marg, New Delhi 110 003. *Tel: (011) 2436 3030; fax: (011) 2436 0484.* **In UK**. *Tel: (0800) 962 096.*

(freephone); fax: (0800) 207 222 9696.
In USA. *Tel: (800) 223 6800 (toll-free), (212) 752 6565; fax: (212) 758 7367.*

Rajasthan Tourism Development Corporation (RTDC)
Bikaner House, Pandara Rd, India Gate, New Delhi. *Tel: (011) 2338 1884/2338 9525/ 2338 6069; fax: (011) 2338 2823.*
Hotel Swagatam Campus, near railway station, Jaipur. *Tel: (0141) 202 586/202 152/203 531; fax: (0141) 201 045.*

Taj Group of Hotels
Luxury/palace hotels in Delhi, Agra, Jaipur, Udaipur.
Taj Mahal Hotel, Apollo Bunder, Mumbai. *Tel: (022) 202 3366; fax: (022) 287 2711.*
In UK. *Tel: (0800) 282699; fax: 207 834 8629.*
In USA. *Tel (toll-free): (800) 458 8825; fax: (212) 751 4091.*

Welcomgroup/Sheraton
Luxury/palace hotels in Delhi, Agra and Jaipur, including heritage properties.
Maurya Sheraton, Diplomatic Enclave, New Delhi 110 021. *Tel: (011) 2611 2233; fax: (011) 2611 3333).*
In UK. *Tel: (0800) 325 3535 (freephone).*
In USA. *Tel: (800) 325 3535 (toll-free); fax: (512) 835 2349.*

The colonial Oberoi Maidens Hotel, one of Delhi's oldest

Heritage hotels

There are over 100 official heritage hotels in India, of which the vast bulk are in Rajasthan. The state also has over 600 forts and castles, over 1,000 palaces, and numerous royal mansions and *havelis* ripe for conversion. A massive development programme with heavy government subsidies is underway. The current brochure lists those in operation, and a list of properties for anyone interested in investing.

Among those already operational are some of the world's finest palace hotels. With much fabulous atmosphere, it seems a shame to stay elsewhere.

Interior of a guest room, Samode Haveli, Jaipur

Mid-range hotels

There is a real shortage of hotels in the Western 3- to 4-star category at a non-expense account price. There are a few, in the US $30/70 (single/double) price range, just below the luxury tax category. The architecture and range of facilities vary, but all are clean, comfortable and well-run. Book well in advance during high season. Some of the better ones are listed below.

Delhi: Oberoi Maidens (Oberoi Hotels), Ambassador (Taj Group); **Agra**: Novotel Agra, *tel: (0562) 2368282*; Amar, *tel: (0562) 2331885*; **Bharatpur**: Forest Lodge (ITDC), *tel: (05644) 222760*; **Jaipur**: Narain Niwas Palace, *tel: (0141) 2561291*, Samode Haveli (private), *tel: (0141) 2632407*; **Jaisalmer**: Bhanwar Niwas, *tel: (02992) 259323*; **Jodhpur**: Ajit Bhawan (private), *tel: (0291) 2511410*; **Sariska**: Hotel Sariska Palace (private), *tel: (0144) 241322*; **Udaipur**: Shikarbadi (private), *tel: (0294) 2583200*; Anand Bhawan (RTDC), *tel: (0294) 2523256*.

Tourist bungalows

Tourist bungalows date back to the Raj when a chain of government guest houses was set up for travelling administrators. These days, the architecture is usually mundane, very few are bungalows, but in some of the smaller towns, they really are the best on offer. In most places, however, they are being overtaken by a constantly changing flow of other smaller, pleasant guesthouses. Run by the **State Tourism Development Corporation**, tourist bungalows exist in almost every town and city in Rajasthan; they provide very reasonably priced lodging with showers and fans that usually work, and they are easy to find in a strange city.

On the other hand, most are sloppily run, and the cleanliness and food could definitely be improved. Prices vary from about Rs1,000–1,300 a night, dependent on location, type of room and facilities.

Other cheap options

You will need to do your homework to find other cheap alternatives. There are a great many cheap and very cheap hotels and guesthouses around. Some are wonderful, others poorly run but with such great atmosphere you can forgive them almost anything. Ask other travellers for suggestions. The *rickshaw-wallahs* will try to steer you away from places that don't pay commission. Don't believe them when they say a place is full, or has gone downhill. On the other hand, if it really has, go and see their suggested place. It may be run by a cousin, but they may have a good idea of what travellers want.

Always inspect the room before you agree to take it, including testing such basics as the flush, lights and fan, and making sure the bed has sufficient clean sheets. If there is anything wrong, ask for a handyman or cleaner to be sent up. You can usually get things sorted if you are persistent. Certain facilities, such as laundry, are available absolutely everywhere.

Ultra-cheap

The rather grim 'Indian' hotels are probably best avoided unless you are totally broke. A number of cheaper hotels also offer some dormitory accommodation, and almost every railway station has retiring rooms, with dormitory beds as well as private rooms. These are very handy if you are arriving late or leaving early. They are very popular and must be booked. Many of the larger temples run pilgrim hostels. They are usually clean, and although the accommodation is spartan and the rules strict, the cost is minimal.

Home stays

Run by the RTDC, this programme, which places travellers as paying guests in a family home, is spreading rapidly and proving highly popular. The accommodation is usually comfortable, and you have an excellent opportunity to get to know the local people.

Ask the RTDC or local tourist offices for complete details.

Hotel pools provide cool pleasure

On business

During the Raj, India was used as a dumping ground for British goods. At Independence, Nehru instituted a series of Five Year Plans, designed to make India as self-sufficient as possible. They have succeeded spectacularly. India can feed herself, and has a broad-based national industry. The range of products, from heavy machinery to domestic goods, has risen sharply through the years, and industry constantly strives to better the existing quality. Today, India is renowned as a world leader in software technology.

Modern glass and steel architecture reflects the corporate culture of India

The last few years have seen a massive policy swing. The rupee has become partially convertible and India is cutting the red tape and opening its doors to international business, although the emphasis is on investment, not imports. There is a vast and very cheap workforce, a huge range of traditional Indian goods which could be adapted for a Western market, and an increasingly large Indian middle class, looking to the West for new ways of spending money.

Business etiquette

Indians can usually pigeonhole people easily and are uncomfortable with unknown Westerners, so take a good supply of business cards and answer their questions to put them at ease. The system is hierarchical, and the trappings of authority will help you maintain a necessary image, as will a formal approach. Western-style informality leaves people uncomfortable and floundering. Women, if professional in their attitude, should have no problems in doing business, and will often be dealing with other Indian women.

Difficulties

The bureaucracy is stuck somewhere in the 19th century. It is cumbersome, infuriating and often totally unnecessary – but it does work, eventually. If you become totally bogged down, take an Indian intermediary to do the negotiating on your behalf.

There is corruption, but it is possible to do business legally. You may be faced with two sets of figures, white money (the price on the invoice), and black money (the real price, or undeclared top-up). The government is trying hard to crack down, with harsh penalties for both parties concerned.

Finally, Indians are very polite. They won't admit they haven't understood, will tell you only what they think you want to hear, and will not argue even if they think you are wrong (although they may go and do what they wanted anyway). Always check things several times and put everything in writing.

Business media

There are four main English-language business papers, the daily *Economic Times* and *Financial Times*, and the bi-monthly *Business India* and *Business Today*. The satellite television channels, BBC World, CNN, Star, CNBC and ZEE TV all do Asian business updates. *(See also p182.)*

Business services

All high-level and government business is conducted in English. Interpreters between all Indian languages and most mainstream world languages are available in Delhi and, to a lesser extent, in Jaipur. Elsewhere, you would do best to take someone with you who can translate. Delhi and Jaipur both have specialist business hotels, with full secretarial facilities, but most luxury hotels offer some services.

The Pragati Maidan exhibition ground in Delhi can house conferences from 15 to 11,000 people. The B M Birla Auditorium in Jaipur can also handle large groups. All the 5-star hotels offer small-scale conference facilities.

Aastha Polylingual and Outsourcing Services, H. No. 308, Munirka, new Delhi 110 067. *Tel: 91-09871234984/91-989178110.*

Pragati Maidan, Bhairon Rd, New Delhi. *Tel: (011) 2337 1529/2337 5254.*

Communications

For **Telephones**, *see p185*. Public fax and telex machines are available in most hotels, the central post office and telecommunications centres, as well as most market places. Because the internal phones are so difficult, the lines are so bad and the possibilities of mislaid/forgotten messages so great even if you do get through, it is worth using a fax or telex to make or confirm any arrangements. Several courier companies have offices in Delhi and Jaipur.

DHL Worldwide Express, D-1 Street, Ashirwad, Green Park, New Delhi 110 016. *Tel: 91-11-6854068.*

Fed-Ex, Flat 8, Balaji Estate, Kalkaji, New Delhi 110 019. *Tel: (011) 628 5911; fax: (011) 628 5915.*

Office Hours

See p183.

Further Information

Confederation of Indian Industries (CII), 23/26 Institutional Area, Lodi Rd, New Delhi 110 003. *Tel: (011) 2462 9994; fax: (011) 2463 3168/2462 6149.*

Federation of Indian Chambers of Commerce and Industry (FICCI), Federation House, Tansen Marg, New Delhi 110 001. *Tel: (011) 2373 8760; fax: (011) 2372 1504.*

PHD Chambers of Commerce, PHD House, Hauz Khas, Opp Asian Games Village, New Delhi 110 016. *Tel: (011) 2686 3801; fax: (011) 2685 7749.*

Practical Guide

Arriving

Most people fly into Delhi. Northern India is landlocked and its three international borders – with Pakistan, Nepal and Bhutan – are traversed by air and land. There are good road and rail links with most other areas of India, and Delhi, Agra, Jaipur, Jaisalmer (three flights per week), Jodhpur and Udaipur are all equipped with domestic airports offering regular scheduled services.

By air

Air India (international) and Indian Airlines (domestic) are both state-run airlines. Many major international airlines also fly into Delhi, most offering good deals, so shop around. Remember to re-confirm all international flights at least 72 hours before departure.

Domestic services were recently deregulated, and there is a growing number of operators who are challenging the position of the long-established Indian Airlines. Standards are improving, but internal flights can be pretty hit or miss, with regular cancellations, over-booking, and delays.

Few Western travel agents are prepared to risk making the booking without a disclaimer. Wait until you arrive, and use a local travel agent who should know what's happening. Indian Airlines offer a US $750, 21-day unlimited travel pass, useful if you are planning to cover the entire subcontinent.

Indira Gandhi Airport

This is India's main international airport. There are currency exchange counters in the baggage reclaim hall, expensive duty-free shops on arrival and departure, and tourist information and hotel booking desks in the arrivals hall.

The easiest transport into town is by pre-paid taxi – get a ticket from a booth in the arrivals hall. There are also very cheap, but slow buses, again bookable before you leave the terminal building. On departure, your baggage must be security checked and sealed, and you must have paid your departure tax.

The international terminal is 23km southwest of the city; the domestic terminal is 8km closer. Airport information: *Tel: (011) 2565 2050.*

Departure tax

There is no airport tax on domestic services; the Rs 500 tax on international flights is now added to the ticket price at the point of sale. There should be nothing further to pay at the airport.

Camping

There are few facilities for camping in or near the towns, and accommodation is so cheap, it really isn't worth it. All camping equipment is supplied during desert safaris.

Children

See pp160–61.

Climate

The tourist season runs from mid-September to April, peaking from November to March. It can be chilly in Delhi, though hot and sunny through the day. The desert can feel bitterly cold at night.

Through May and June, the temperature climbs steadily under a sweltering sun to almost unbearable levels until early July, when the monsoon arrives with torrential rains, thunderstorms and, all too frequently, floods. This lasts to early September. The desert collects few of the monsoon rains, but the season is characterised instead by high winds and sandstorms.

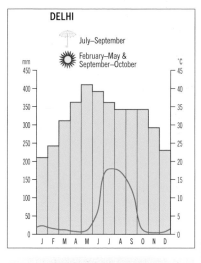

DELHI

July–September

February–May &
September–October

Weather Conversion Chart
25.4mm = 1 inch
°F = 1.8 x °C + 32

Clothing

Clothes should be portable, durable, comfortable and all-encompassing. Women should avoid short skirts, shorts (culottes are a good alternative), and anything sleeveless; men can wear baggy shorts but may need long trousers for temple visiting. Loose-fitting clothes in natural fibres or mixes, such as cotton or poly-cotton, are best suited to the heat. Dress is usually informal, but take at least one reasonable outfit (including a tie for men) for smarter restaurants. You will probably need a lightweight jacket or sweater for evenings. Long sleeves and trousers help fend off mosquitoes. Wear comfortable shoes or sandals that allow your feet to breathe.

It is easy and incredibly cheap to get laundry done, but your clothes will take a hammering. If you have anything fragile, wash it yourself. Try to take things that don't need ironing.

It is possible to get clothes made in hours. The Indian *shalwar kameez* (pyjama suit for women) is ideally suited to the climate and very comfortable.

Conversion tables

India uses the metric system. There is a slightly different method of counting high numbers. One lakh is 100,000 (written as 1,00,000); one crore is 10,000,000 (written as 1,00,00,000).

Crime

See Security, *p185.*

Customs regulations

200 cigarettes, 1 litre of alcohol, and gifts to the value of Rs 600 are allowed into the country. Declare more than US $10,000 and any expensive electrical items, such as camcorders and computers, which will be checked on departure. Clearance is needed for the export of antiques, and export of animal

products such as crocodile and snake skin. (*Check with Ministry of Environment & Forests, tel: (011) 2388 4556.*)

Documents

A valid passport and visa are needed. Apply in person in your home country or expect delays. Allow up to two weeks. Most tourist visas are valid for six months. Check the current situation with the Indian Embassy in your country. Visa applications can be made at the embassies below:

Embassies
Indian embassies abroad
Australia
3–5 Moonah Place, Yarralumla, ACT 2600. *Tel: (62) 733 3999/939 7000.*
Canada
10 Springfield Rd, Ottawa. K1M 1C9. *Tel: (613) 744 3751;* 325 Howe St, 1st Fl, Vancouver, British Columbia. *Tel: (604) 662 8811.*
New Zealand
10th Fl, Princess Tower, 180 Molesworth St, Wellington. *Tel: (4) 73 6390.*
UK
India House, Aldwych, London WC2B 4NA. *Tel: (020) 7836 8484.*
USA
2107 Massachusetts Ave NW, Washington DC 20008. *Tel: (202) 939 9806.*

Foreign embassies in India
Australia
1/50-G Shantipath, Delhi. *Tel: (011) 2668 8823.*
Canada
7/8 Shantipath, Delhi. *Tel: (011) 2687 6500.*

New Zealand
50-N Nyaya Marg, Delhi. *Tel: (011) 2688 3170.*
UK
50 Shantipath, Delhi. *Tel: (011) 2687 2161.*
USA
Shantipath, Delhi. *Tel: (011) 2419 8000.*

Electricity

220–240 volts. Most plugs take two round pins. Power cuts are frequent in places, but short-lived. Take a torch.

Emergency telephone numbers
Police: *100*
Fire: *101*
Ambulance: *102*

Health

India is home to many diseases. Follow the advice given by your doctor or travel company, take the shots, carry a good medical kit, including sterile needles. If something does go wrong, don't shrug it off, but don't panic. Few travellers suffer more than minor stomach upsets.

AIDS and Hepatitis B

Both diseases are widely prevalent. Stay celibate or take a good supply of condoms, and use them.

Inoculations

There are no statutory requirements. However, it is sensible to have inoculations for typhoid, tetanus, polio, tuberculosis, yellow fever, meningitis A and C (for Delhi and the north) and hepatitis A. The cholera vaccine is ineffectual, so is not recommended.

Hospitals and doctors

The quality of medical care varies enormously, although the standard of medical training is good. Most hotels have an English-speaking doctor on call. If you need hospitalisation, insist on one of the big teaching hospitals or a private clinic, which are as good as any in the world. Ambulances are on call. Insist on using your own needles and do everything short of dying before you have a transfusion of local blood. Ask your friends to help and contact your embassy. Some have blood banks, others keep a register of clean donors.

Malaria

Malaria is endemic and can kill. You must take prophylaxis. Check with a good travel clinic or tropical diseases hospital. Start two weeks before you leave and keep taking the pills for four weeks after you get home. If you show flu-like symptoms at any time within the next six months, ask for a malaria test. The carrier, the female anopheles mosquito, only comes out at night. The best prevention is to avoid being bitten, so cover up well, use a good repellent, spray the room, use a coil and, if possible, a mosquito net.

Stomach bugs

These are almost obligatory, but most are minor and will disappear within a day or so. Eat basic food such as dry toast, *chapatis* and yoghurt, and drink plenty of water, with a little sugar and salt to help replace essential minerals. If the problem lasts more than a couple of days, consult a doctor.

Never, never drink water unless from a sealed mineral water bottle or one you have sterilised yourself. This includes ice and street-stall fruit juices (diluted with tap water). Check out any restaurant for basic cleanliness, and wash your own hands before you touch food. Stick to well wrapped, and fresh-cooked, hot foods. Never eat any fruit you can't peel.

Sunburn and heatstroke

Much of this area is desert, and all of it is very hot. It is easy to burn and dehydrate. Wear a hat, use sunglasses and a high-factor sun block, and carry water with you. Drink far more than you think you should need. First symptoms of heatstroke (overload of the cooling system) include a headache, nausea and blurred vision. Get into a cold bath and call a doctor.

Rabies

Don't touch any animals, domestic or wild. Rabies is one of a host of infections they may carry. Should you get bitten or scratched, insist on full rabies treatment immediately. If you wait until symptoms develop, it's too late. If travelling more than 24 hours away from medical help, get immunised before leaving.

Insurance

Good, comprehensive travel insurance is essential. Too many things can go wrong here. Your policy should cover air evacuation, third-party liability, legal assistance, loss of possessions (including finances and passports), cancellation and/or delay of travel. Adventure sports and motorcycles are rarely covered by standard policies.

Language

India has 18 official languages (and about 1,652 dialects), of which Hindi is the most widely spoken, especially in this region. English is the language of government. A few words of Hindi can be useful and will always be appreciated, but almost everybody speaks some English, and if they don't, the person eavesdropping will willingly help out.

Newspapers have a wide audience in India

Media

India is very media-oriented. The main national English-language dailies include the *Times of India*, *Hindustan Times*, *Hindu*, *Indian Express* and *Statesman*. All major cities have their own English-language daily and there are numerous weekly or monthly news government magazines. Doordarshan is the official TV channel with English, Hindi and regional broadcasts, but there are a host of other channels. Satellite and cable channels are available in most good hotels. Numerous local and national radio stations broadcast in a range of languages including English. International newspapers, *Time* and *Newsweek*, are available a few days late and are very expensive.

Money matters

Currency

The rupee is divided into units of 100 paise (rarely used except as *baksheesh*). Keep a good supply of small notes and coins. No one ever has change. Check all notes carefully. If badly torn, they become invalid, and can be changed at a bank. The Rs 1,000 is the highest.

Exchange facilities

It is legal to import up to 5,000 rupees, but no export of rupees is permitted. There are 24-hour exchange facilities at the airport. Change money at hotels or agencies where possible, or use the ATMs which are springing up in the cities. Not all banks handle foreign exchange, and the procedure can be time-consuming and wearisome. The black market rate isn't worth the risk. Keep your exchange forms. You will need one to change money back into hard currency, or pay for hotel rooms or air tickets in rupees.

Cheques and credit cards

For safety, use well-known brands of US dollar or pounds sterling traveller's cheques. Counter clerks won't change anything they don't recognise. Major credit cards are widely accepted on the luxury circuit. Elsewhere, they are useless, so always carry enough cash to support yourself. India is still primarily a cash economy. An emergency supply of a few (cash) dollars can be helpful if you need money away from the major cities.

If you need to transfer money quickly, you can use the MoneyGram℠ Money Transfer service. For more details call *Freephone 0800 8971 8971* (UK).

Prices

The luxury end of the market works to international standards and prices (usually quoted in US dollars), and attracts a high luxury tax, on top of the usual sales tax. Out of package-tour land, prices plummet to Indian levels, which are rock-bottom. A few shops, restaurants, hotels and markets all work to fixed pricing. Elsewhere, you must haggle, with the first price quoted based on what they think you can afford. You may pay more than an Indian would, but it will still be a bargain for you.

National Holidays

26 January Republic Day
15 August Independence Day
2 October Mahatma Gandhi's birthday
25 December Christmas Day
There are a great many movable festivals, only some of which count as official holidays. The main ones are listed in Festivals (*see pp24–5*).

Opening hours

Opening hours tend to be flexible, so these are a guide only. Many banks stay open all week, and have ATM facilities.

Banks: Mon–Fri 10am–2pm; Sat 10am–noon.
Government offices: Mon–Fri 9.30am–5pm.
Post Offices: Mon–Fri 10am–5pm; Sat 10am–3pm.
Shops: Mon–Sat 9.30/10am–7.30pm (small shops and bazaars often open until at least 8pm).

Organised tours

Huge numbers of Western tour operators offer tours including Delhi, Agra and Jaipur; fewer take you further into Rajasthan, and very few indeed stir off the well-trodden path around the half-dozen major cities. Most of them stay at the same few palace hotels, and do pretty much the same things. Shop around for price, and also look at how long they are likely to give you at each stop.

Once in India, everybody is prepared to offer every conceivable version, from the coach trip to the luxury custom tour, even if it is not in their brochure. For day or half-day tours, stick with the tourist office, who will either have a coach tour, or can provide you with your own guide. For longer tours, use a reputable operator, such as Thomas Cook (*see p185*). (*For Off-beat Safaris, see p146; for the Palace on Wheels, see p29.*)

Pharmacies

Pharmacies are readily available. They work long hours, but don't rely on a rota-system for 24-hour service. Out of hours, try the nearest hospital or clinic. You can get local versions of all common medicines, but specialised medicines may be hard to find.

LANGUAGE

USEFUL WORDS		USEFUL PHRASES	
brother	bhai	do you speak English?	Angrezi aati hai?
car, train, vehicle	gaari	how much is this?	yeh kitne ka hai?
child's nursemaid	ayah	hurry up	jaldi karo
come/go	aao/jao	I don't want it	mujhe nahin chahiye
elephant	hathi	I would like	mujhe chahiye
garden	bagh	It's expensive	mehnga hai
government	sarkar	let's go	chalo
Indian sweets	mitthai	lower the price	kam karo
less/more	thora/zyada	never mind	koi baat nahin
mansion	haveli	please	kripya
near/far	paas/door	thank you	dhanyavad
raw	kutcha	what is this?	yeh kya hai?
reply	jawab		
ripe or solid, reliable	pukka		
soap	sabun		
temple	mandir		
water	pani	**NUMBERS**	
what	kya	1 ek	6 chhe
when	kab	2 do	7 saat
where	kahan	3 teen	8 aath
worship	puja	4 char	9 nau
yes/no	ji haan/ji nahin	5 paanch	10 dus

Places of worship

There are Hindu and Jain temples and mosques in abundance. All the major towns have at least one Christian church. There is a synagogue in Delhi. Look in the phone directory or ask the hotel reception for details.

Police

Indian police are not the world's most sympathetic. Some are fine, but there is a lot of corruption.

If you need to claim on your insurance, you will have to produce an FIR (First Information Report) registered with the police. Dress as smartly as possible, take someone with you as a witness, and make sure there is a written record of everything. If in doubt, or if you are arrested, get word to your embassy immediately.

Post

Use a fax for urgent correspondence. Speed Post claims to guarantee delivery in Europe, USA, and most countries in 48 to 72 hours. Stamps are sold at most hotels as well as post offices. For *poste restante*, underline the surname as things can get lost by misfiling. Sending parcels can be really time-consuming.

Public transport *See pp26–30.*

Security

India is fairly safe. There is a lot of petty crime such as pick-pocketing, and most women face a degree of irritating hassle, but violent crime is rare. Nevertheless, travellers are advised to stay alert.

Always use a money belt for valuables and cash. Keep some emergency cash, a record of your traveller's cheques and credit cards, some spare passport photos, and a photocopy of the crucial pages of your passport (including the visa) somewhere separate. Don't leave baggage unattended at any time. Watch out for sleight of hand tricks when other people are handling your money. Don't always trust other travellers. Above all, don't do drugs, and never carry anything through Customs for anyone. The penalties are harsh these days.

Student and youth travel

Most Western tourists to India are young. Indian Airlines do a 25 per cent youth discount. There are no other youth discounts, but they aren't really necessary since prices are so low.

Insurance and attention to hygiene are crucially important to budget travellers. Ensure someone always knows your whereabouts in case of emergency.

Telephones

The internal phone system is extremely frustrating. Avoid it where possible.

Phone booths have sprung up almost everywhere recently, usually in the back room of a small shop. Look for yellow signs saying ISO (local), STD (long-distance), and/or ISD (international). Metered machines show how much you are spending. Pay at the end. If you need to book through the operator, you have a choice of regular (normally up to one hour wait) or lightning calls (still up to 30 minutes wait, and many times more expensive). Many charge cards, such as AT&T, BT and Mercury, are valid. *For telex/fax, see p177.*

Thomas Cook
India
Delhi Rishyamook Building, 85–A Panchkuin Rd, New Delhi. *Tel: (011) 2374 7404.*
Hotel Imperial, Janpath, New Delhi. *Tel: (011) 2336 8561.*
Near platform No. 12, Ajmeri Gate side, New Delhi rly stn. *Tel: (011) 2321 1819.*
Indira Gandhi International Airport, Terminal 2. *Tel: (011) 2565 2021/2011/3439.*
C-33 Connaught Place, Inner Circle, New Delhi. *Tel: (011) 2335 6571–79.*
717/718 International Trade Tower, Nehru Place, New Delhi. *Tel: (011) 2642 3035.*
Rajasthan Flat No. AB-2 (102) Jaipur Towers, 1st Fl, Mirza Ismail Rd, Jaipur. *Tel: (0141) 2360940/2360801.*

Thomas Cook in India operate a wide variety of tours, both day trips and longer. They customise tours for individuals, business travellers, conferences and incentive groups. Thomas Cook's website, at *www.thomascook.com,* provides details of Thomas Cook's travel services.

Time

GMT + 5 hours 30 minutes. When it is

noon in Delhi, it is 6.30am in London, 1.30am in New York and 4.30pm in Sydney, Australia.

Tipping

Tipping, as opposed to *baksheesh* (*see p31*), is customary at more up-market hotels and restaurants, although many include a service charge, and a few rupees is plenty. Tip hotel porters and suchlike about Rs10–20. Station porters and taxi drivers officially work to set rates, but will always try to over-inflate the price.

If you have had to haggle for anything, don't spoil the effect by giving in to demands for more. Be generous, but also spare a thought for other impecunious travellers coming behind you.

Toilets

Most public places have Indian-style long-drop toilets, although some have a few Western-style seats as well. The luxury market lives up to its name with splendid facilities, and hot and cold running assistants. At the other extreme, toilets are scenes from hell. Public toilets are few and far between. Wherever you find something vaguely hygienic, grab the opportunity. Always carry with you your own supply of toilet paper and soap.

Tourist information in India

Government of India Tourist Office
88 Janpath, New Delhi.
Tel: (011) 2332 0005/8.
India Tourism Development Corporation
L-Block, Connaught Place, New Delhi.
Tel: (011) 2332 0331/2332 2336.

Delhi Tourism Development Corporation
N-36, Connaught Place, New Delhi.
Tel: (011) 2331 3636.
Rajasthan Tourism Development Corporation
Bikaner House, Pandara Rd, India Gate, New Delhi.
Tel: (011) 2338 1884/2338 9525.
Hotel Swagatam Campus, near the railway station, Jaipur.
Tel: (0141) 2202 761.
Uttar Pradesh Tourist Office
Chandralok Bldg, 36 Janpath, New Delhi. *Tel: (011) 2332 2251/2371 1296.*
64 Taj Rd, Agra. *Tel: (0562) 2360517.*

Websites:
delhitourism.com; delhitourism.nic.com; up-tourism.com; rajasthan.gov.in; rajasthandiary.com; rajasthan-tour.com

Travellers with disabilities

Life is not impossible, but it is very difficult indeed. The airlines provide wheelchairs, the better hotels have lifts, and a very few up-market international chains provide basic facilities. Elsewhere, there is no provision.

On the plus side, labour is very cheap and the Indians are, by nature, kind. Expect to be almost totally reliant on muscle power.

For more information, contact *RADAR* (the Royal Association for Disability and Rehabilitation), 12 City Forum, 250 City Rd, London EC1V 8AF. *Tel: (020) 7250 3222; fax: (020) 7250 0212,* or SATH (Society for Accessible Travel and Hospitality), 347 Fifth Ave, Ste 610, New York, NY 10016. *Tel: (212) 447 7284; fax: (212) 725 8253.*

Sustainable Travel

MAKE A DIFFERENCE WHEN YOU TRAVEL

The Travel Foundation is a UK charity that cares for the places we love to visit.

By following this simple advice, you can get more out of your holiday – and help make a positive difference to the lives of the people and places you visit. You can also help to ensure there are special places for us all to visit – for generations to come!

To find out more about The Travel Foundation and what you can do, please visit *www.thetravelfoundation.org.uk*.

What you can do:

- Remove any packaging from items (and recycle if possible) before you go on holiday.
- Booking excursions that use local suppliers or using local guides and taxis will enrich your holiday experience and help support the local economy.
- Hire a car only if you need to. Using public transport, bicycles and walking are environmentally-friendlier alternatives.
- Respect local culture and traditions. Ensure your dress and behaviour is appropriate for the places you visit. Ask permission before taking photographs of people or their homes.
- Turn down/off heating or air conditioning when not required.

Switch off lights and turn the television off rather than leave on standby.

- Please don't have your photograph taken with any 'wild' animals (such as lion or tiger cubs, chimpanzees or exotic birds). They are taken from the wild when young, often mistreated and killed when too big or difficult to handle.
- Do use water sparingly. Take showers instead of baths and inform staff if you are happy to re-use towels and bed linen rather than replace daily.
- Please don't pick flowers and plants or collect pebbles, seashells, coral or starfish. Leave them for others to enjoy.
- Please don't buy products made from endangered plants or animals, including hardwoods, ivory, corals, reptiles or turtles. If in doubt – don't buy.
- Do buy locally-made products – shopping in locally-owned outlets and treating yourself to local food and drink is a great way to get into the holiday spirit and benefits local families.
- Coral is extremely fragile. Please don't step on or remove it and avoid kicking up sand.

the travel foundation
caring for places we love to visit

ACKNOWLEDGEMENTS
Thomas Cook wishes to thank the photographers, picture libraries and other organisations for the loan of the photographs reproduced in this book, to whom copyright in the photographs belongs.

David Henley/CPA Media 7, 9, 10, 12, 13, 14, 15, 16a, 16b, 17, 23, 25, 27a, 27b, 29b, 34, 40b, 45, 46, 48, 49, 50, 52, 54a, 54b, 56a, 59, 60, 64, 65, 66, 68b, 69, 71, 72, 73, 74, 77a, 77b, 82, 84, 88, 92, 104a, 107, 112a, 114, 123, 128, 131, 132, 139, 142, 143, 144a, 144b, 145, 149, 152, 158, 162, 163, 173, 175, 176, 182
David Tipling/Alamy 126
Dynamic Graphics Group/Creatas/Alamy 127

The remaining pictures are held in the AA PHOTO LIBRARY and were taken by DOUGLAS CORRANCE.

Travellers **Delhi, Agra & Rajasthan**

Feedback Form

Please help us improve future editions by taking part in our reader survey. Every returned form will be acknowledged. To show our appreciation we will send you a voucher entitling you to £1 off your next *Travellers* guide or any other Thomas Cook guidebook ordered direct from Thomas Cook Publishing. Just take a few minutes to complete and return this form to us.

We'd also be glad to hear of your comments, updates or recommendations on places we cover or you think that we ought to cover.

1. Which of the following tempted you into buying your *Travellers* guide:
   (Please tick as many as appropriate)

   a) the price ☐

   b) the cover ☐

   c) the content ☐

   d) other _____

2. What do you think of:

   a) the cover design _____

   b) the design and layout styles within the book _____

   c) the content_____

   d) the maps _____

3. Please tell us about any features that in your opinion could be changed, improved or added in future editions of the book or any other comments you would like to make concerning this book _____

   _____

   _____

   _____

   _____

4. What is the single most useful/helpful aspect of this book?_____

   _____

5. Have you purchased other *Travellers* guides in the series?

    a) yes   ☐

    b) no   ☐

    If yes, please specify which titles _____

6. Would you purchase other *Travellers* guides?

    a) yes   ☐

    b) no   ☐

    If no, please specify why not _____

Your age category: ☐ under 21   ☐ 21–30   ☐ 31–40   ☐ 41–50   ☐ 51+

Mr/Mrs/Miss/Ms/Other

Surname_____ Initials_____

Full address (please include postal or zip code):_____

_____

_____

Daytime telephone number: _____

E-mail address:_____

Please detach this page and send it to: **The Series Editor, *Travellers* guides,
Thomas Cook Publishing, PO Box 227, The Thomas Cook Business Park,
Units 15–16, Coningsby Road, Peterborough PE3 8SB, United Kingdom.**

Alternatively, you can e-mail us at: ***books@thomascook.com***